BULLETPROOF
MARRIAGE

To Angelia
+ Andres

BULLETPROOF MARRIAGE

SHIELDING YOUR MARRIAGE AGAINST DIVORCE

Renato and Cristiane Cardoso

GRUPO NELSON
Una división de Thomas Nelson Publishers
Desde 1798

NASHVILLE   MÉXICO DF.   RÍO DE JANEIRO

Originally published in Portuguese under the title: *Casamento blindado*

© Thomas Nelson Brasil, Vida Melhor Editora SA, 2012
Rua Nova Jeresalém, 345, Bonsucesso Rio de Janeiro, RJ, 21402-325
www.thomasnelson.com.br

© Textos: Renato Cardoso, Cristiane Cardoso

Names and identifying details of some people mentioned in this book have been
changed to protect their privacy.

The websites and organizations recommended in this book are intended as resources
for the reader. These websites and organizations are not intended in any way to be or to
imply an endorsement on behalf of Grupo Nelson, nor does the publisher vouch for their
content for the life of this book.

ISBN: 978-0-71802-597-7

Printed in the United States of America

15 16 17 18 19 RRD 7 6 5 4 3 2 1

DEDICATION

To all the couples who value their marriage enough to bulletproof it. And to those wise single people who know that is better to prevent something than have to heal it.

RENATO AND CRISTIANE CARDOSO

To Patricia + Ahmet

CONTENTS

PART II
EMOTION VS. REASON

PART III
TAKING LOVE APART AND PUTTING IT
BACK TOGETHER

PART IV

BULLETPROOFING IT

 # PREFACE

"Defence! Defence!"

As you start to read this preface, you would probably expect to find references to basketball, a sport that has brought me great achievement, struggle, joy, conflict, and reward. To be honest, though, I would rather speak about another area of my life that has also brought achievement, struggle, joy, conflict, and reward, but one that has been much deeper and more meaningful: my marriage. And to be even more honest: if it hadn't been for the strength of my marriage to Cristiane, it's likely I would have a lot less to talk about, including anything in my life as an athlete.

Cristiane and I have been married for over thirty years, yet we have known each other for nearly four decades. I know this sounds like a cliché, but I cannot help thinking—and I am sure you will agree—that it seems like we've always been together. Imagine all the things that can happen in a lifetime—sunny days and perfect weather, but also rainy days and storms. It's all about having a well-grounded relationship that can stand up to the stormy winds of life that try to bring it all down.

If I were to go back forty years ago, when I was more naïve (when I didn't believe in the Easter Bunny), I would have said that every problem in a marriage could be solved with love. Obviously, it is a key element to any relationship—no couple can stay together and be happy without love—but I can assure you that there are many more aspects to marriage that come into play.

I can simply begin by explaining how my wife, Cristiane, was able to give up her college degree only three months before graduation and move to Europe with me, where I started playing six months after our wedding. In those first weeks, she supported both of us financially, when the team I was playing on started the season on the wrong foot. No matter how much I had to train or concentrate on my game, Cristiane never dropped the ball at home. Without her, I probably would have given up. With her, I returned home a champion a few years later.

In basketball (okay, I am talking about basketball after all), no self-respecting team will get results unless they work as a team. The one who scores a point also turns around to play defence in order to protect the rest of the team. In the United States, fans shout, "Defence! Defence!" I've come to realize that this works in marriage exactly the same way. When we love, we advance, progress, and win, but it's also about being concerned about protecting not only our spouse but our relationship as well. Out of respect for Cristiane, I stopped bringing fans along with us on the bus. It wasn't just about sparing her the embarrassment; it was also about preserving our unity, our love, and our relationship.

This is why I was thrilled when I was asked to write the Preface for Renato and Cristiane Cardoso's book. I've read a few books on marriage and heard about others, but this is the first time I've found one that goes to the heart of the issue: the one who truly loves will bulletproof his marriage. Bullet-proofing is just that—setting in place all the defences that will block anything that could potentially jeopardize the relationship. This includes not just external attacks but also those that come from within: put-downs for silly things, crises (they always appear), the lack of humility to know how to lovingly give in (or stand your ground in love), an inability to adapt to each other's strengths and defects, blackmailing, emotional games . . . and the list goes on and on.

Renato and Cristiane learned these things after many years of couple's counseling, but their best training was the school of life. This is where they discovered the power of bulletproofing their marriage, which becomes stronger and more solid when it is based on Christian principles and values. And now they share these experiences and guidance in this book. It is a great opportunity for those who have discovered that their marriage is vulnerable and needs to be shielded, as well as for those who have already bulletproofed their marriage and know the importance of strengthening that protection. Read it and bulletproof your marriage too.

Oscar Schmidt
Hall of Famer and Brazil's all-time greatest
basketball player, married to Cristiane and
father of Felipe and Stephanie

INTRODUCTION

People don't get married out of hate. I have never heard of anyone asking for a person's hand in marriage by saying, "I hate you! Will you marry me?" People marry for love. Despite that, divorce rates continue to rise each year. In some countries, such as the U.S., half of all marriages end in divorce. In South America more than half of all marriages end up in divorce, and the statistics have increased since 2012. Out of every three marriages, one hits the rocks. And it is going from bad to worse.

It shows that the "love" that binds people together has not been enough to maintain a strong marriage. Scary, isn't it? Just imagine: the love that you have for each other may not be enough when a marriage crisis comes along!

The problem is not a lack of love, but rather a lack of the tools to solve problems that are part and parcel of being a married couple. People get married with virtually no ability to solve problems that arise with married life. For some reason, this is not taught anywhere—at least, not in a clear, practical way it needs to be. In the past, training for marriage came from parents. When marriages were strong and exemplary, children looked to their parents as models of how to act in a relationship. Nowadays, parents are often an example of what not to do . . .

We have another big problem: ignorance of the true meaning of love. I have often heard many frustrated husbands and wives say, "We've fallen out of love. I no longer feel what I felt for him/her."

Others say that their marriage was a mistake, they married the wrong person, they got married too soon, or they were forced into marriage because of a particular circumstance, such as an unplanned pregnancy. The truth is, more often than not, married people are unhappy because of what they are doing wrong, not because they married the wrong person. People do so many wrong things in their relationships. They accumulate problems without ever solving them, which leads to a suf-focated, broken and helpless love—that is, if it isn't killed before it's even born. Good feelings end up giving way to anger, indifference, and even hatred.

But you can salvage your love, and even learn to love someone you have never loved. Pay close attention to what I just said: you can learn to love. The first step is understanding that the only way to love a per-son is to get to know them on a deeper level.

Many make the mistake of viewing love as a feeling. It is correct to say that love produces good feelings, but it is not a feeling. When you meet a person for the first time and feel something good about them, but then do not learn how to love them for who they are, that "love at first sight" will not last very long. Love is not mere feeling. Love is knowing the other person, admiring everything you learn about them, and seeing their flaws in a positive light. We can learn to love anyone or anything, if we make the effort to do it.

For example, let's consider Dian Fossey. The epitaph on her grave-stone reads: "No one loved gorillas more." Dian was an American zoologist, who was famous and respected for her studies of gorillas in Central Africa. Dian lived among the mountain gorillas of Rwanda for many years, until poachers murdered her. She lived in a log cabin, in primitive conditions, and dedicated more than eighteen years of her life to these animals, whom she loved more than anything in life. How did Dian's love for gorillas begin?

At thirty-one, when she went on an African safari, Dian had her first encounter with gorillas and the studies of conservationists who worked for the preservation of the primates. While there she began learning more about them, their behavior, how they communicate with each other, their habits, their diet, their threat of extinction, and much more. Dian is credited for debunking the negative reputation that gorillas gained after the *King Kong* movie depicted them as aggressive and wild animals. Her studies showed that, in reality, these animals are "dignified, highly social, gentle giants, with individual personalities and strong family relationships"—putting them well ahead of many men . . .

My point is that she *learned* to love gorillas. Anyone who loves someone or something initiates that love by gaining knowledge about the object of their love. Some people love animals, others love stars and celestial bodies, others love toy soldiers, and still others love architecture . . . But the love of each one sprang from studying, learning, and becoming knowledgeable about what or whom they loved. Nobody loves what they do not know.

Unfortunately, many couples have never learned to love each other. They got married because of a feeling, passion, or some other circumstance, but they never learned how to study or learn about each other, or discover what makes them happy. When you do not really know another person, it is impossible to love them because you do not know what pleases or annoys them, what their dreams and struggles are, or how they think. That is most likely what will cause you to commit a lot of mistakes in your relationship and cause a continuous stream of problems. These problems will cause you to withdraw from each other, even though you are married and were in love at one time.

If you have been wondering:

- Do I still love my husband/wife?
- Did I marry the wrong person?

- Why is my partner so cold to me?
- Why do we love each other but can't stay together?
- How can I make sure my marriage lasts?
- How can I live with a person who is so difficult?
- Why do our problems go away, but then come back worse than before?
- Is my marriage always going to be about hardships, or will I find happiness one day?

Cheer up! You will learn how to love intelligently and how to be happy with your spouse, even if he (or she) acts like King Kong . . .

THE AUTHORS

Cristiane and I were married in 1991 and have an adopted son. I came from a broken home, which was ruined by infidelity and divorce. My parents were the reason for the outrage I felt in my life when I was only thirteen. At the time, a series of events caused their separation, which was very traumatic for me. I felt like the whole world was crumbling down around me. My father was my hero, but when I learned that he had had an affair, a sense of despair washed over me. I began questioning why all of this had happened. I wanted to die. Driven by this suffering, I found faith and became a believer in the Lord Jesus. Later, my parents also came to faith, and after many years of suffering, their lives were restored as well. I did not learn a religious faith, but one that I was able to use to solve problems. This is why I decided to dedicate my life to sharing what I have learned with others, so that they will be able to overcome their difficulties as well. I cannot keep to myself these insights that literally have saved my life and my parents' lives.

Later, I married Cristiane. Since she was a pastor's daughter, we shared the same goals. On the surface, we had everything for a trouble–free marriage, but it was not that easy. We faced various problems, many of which we will discuss throughout this book.

Strengthening marriages, educating couples and singles, and fighting for fewer marriages to end in divorce became a mission in my life. Today I know that the pain I felt during my teenage years when my parents separated, and later in my marriage, could have been avoided.

If my parents had had access to the information you will receive from this book, they would not have gone through all the hardships they did. If Cristiane and I had known all the things you are about to read in this book before we got married, we would not have caused each other to suffer.

Unfortunately, people suffer because of a lack of knowledge. Nowadays there are schools for all kinds of training, but not for marriage. Even among Christians, there are plenty of theories about love, dating, and marriage, but when the time comes to put these things into practice, people generally do not know what to do. Useful relationship skills and marriage education are rare. So here are two reasons why we dedicate ourselves to passing on this knowledge to other couples: (1) for dating couples and newlyweds to avoid making mistakes that can jeopardize the future of their relationship, and (2) for those who are already in a troubled marriage to learn how to solve problems and live together happily.

Cristiane and I speak from personal experience in our marriage, and from years of counseling other couples. As part of our work across four continents, we have counseled thousands of couples, from teenagers to sexagenarians (never older; it seems that couples in their seventies realize that life is too short to be fighting all the time . . .), and due to high demand, our work with couples has increased in recent years.

In late 2007, our work took us to Texas in the United States. This is where the concept of "The Bulletproof Marriage" course evolved, which resulted in this book. We felt compelled to share our experiences there because of this alarming fact: out of every ten marriages, almost six end in divorce.

The American couples that came to us for counseling had been through multiple relationships and continued to have problems. Many were already in their third, fourth, even fifth marriage, and had clearly not learned anything from their previous relationships. We felt an obligation to help them, to pass on what we had learned. The results helped us to realize that although our experiences and lessons were nothing new, they had a transforming effect in the lives of many couples.

I believe this is due to the unique combination of factors that Cristiane and I have put together: (1) personal experience, (2) experiences we have gained from counseling thousands of couples across four continents, and (3) the use of spiritual wisdom. Let me briefly explain the third factor.

Marriage was God's idea. He decided that man and woman should be "one flesh." Furthermore, the Bible says "God is love."[1] So if we are trying to discover the best way for people to live as a married couple, it is only wise that we return to its origins, where it all began, and to the Source of love. This is why our lessons are based on the wisdom of God—on those things that He determined would work. This does not mean that the objective of this book is to convert you to Christ, if you are not a Christian. Nor will we be referring to the Bible throughout the book, though at times it will be inevitable. However, I must say: without the principles established by God as the foundation for a good marriage, your efforts will be in vain. We have noticed that couples that have embraced this fact are the happiest and the most successful in their efforts to restore and maintain their marriages.

An additional factor in the great success of our teachings is that we focus our help on two main points: solving problems and preventing them from happening again. Most marital problems are recurring. Therefore, it is not enough for you to know how to solve the problems you are now having. You need to cut the problem at its root so it does not come back again in the future. We are certain that if you read this book with an open mind and are willing to at least try to apply the tools

---

[1] 1 John 4:8.

we teach you, you will have a strong and happy marriage. Remember: practice makes perfect.

P.S. Some chapters end with some suggested task, so you can apply what you have learned. Do not underestimate the power of these exercises. We believe that if you are reading this book, it's because you want to see results, but they will only come when you put what you have learned to the test. This is so serious that we invite you to make your efforts public. If you are part of a social network, share the tasks that you are performing so that others can motivate you throughout your journey. Why not start now?

Post your comments on our page www.facebook.com/Bulletproof Marriage so we can track your progress (we have also posted videos on this page to help you with your tasks . . . check them out!). On Twitter, make sure you tweet us @BulletproofMate and add the hashtag *#Bulletproofmarriage* (Facebook also now accepts hashtags).

/BulletproofMarriage

On our Facebook page
fb.com/BulletproofMarriage
post: *Today, I am starting to bulletproof my marriage. #Bulletproofmarriage*

@BulletproofMate

Tweet: Today, I am starting to bulletproof my marriage. *#Bulletproofmarriage @BulletproofMate*

PART I

UNDERSTANDING MARRIAGE

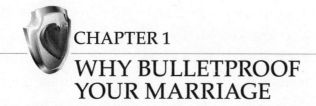

CHAPTER 1

WHY BULLETPROOF YOUR MARRIAGE

Concerned about the rising rate of divorce, some Mexican lawmakers are proposing a new law: renewable marriage contracts. They believe they have found the perfect solution to prevent serious marriages crises, infidelity, and divorce. Every two years, married couples would have the option to reevaluate their relationship and choose whether to remain together and renew their contract or give up and go their separate ways. In addition to signing a temporary contract, the proposal suggests that the bride and groom protect themselves from a potential divorce proceedings. Before marriage, they would have to decide who will have custody of the children and how much alimony would be paid in child support in case of a break-up. The proposal, which is now in Congress, has received broad support from Mexicans who want to end the high cost of divorce and alimony. After all, marriage statistics in Mexico City are bleak: five out of ten marriages end in divorce.

If the law is passed, conversations like this may become common-place between classmates in school:

"Hey, where are you going over the school holidays?" a teenager asks his friend.

"Well, that depends. If my dad renews his marriage contract with my mom at the end of the year, we'll probably go to Disneyland. If not, I'll have to see which one of them wants me, and since my last few report cards have been pretty bad, they'll probably send me to my grandma's . . ."

I don't want to be the bearer of bad news, but here's a fact: marriage as an institution is breaking down under the heavy attack from various elements in society. This Mexican proposal is a symptom of how governments are attempting to cope with high divorce rates. And this is not limited to Mexico. I don't know of a single case in any country, culture, or society in the world where marriage is getting stronger, not even in traditional cultures where religion is highly valued. In the United States, which dictates the cultural trends for the rest of the world, most babies born to women under the age of thirty are born out of wedlock. Some renowned American sociologists have even argued that father figures are not essential in families.

Can you see where we're headed?

Even in places where divorce rates are lower, the numbers barely disguise the truth of what's happening: fewer people are getting married, while increasing numbers are opting for "cohabitation." Consequently, when these couples do separate, it does not count statistically as a divorce. And many who remain together only do so for lack of other options or because of religious pressure, but they continue to be unhappy.

The harsh reality of the situation makes me wonder what things will be like in five, ten, or twenty years. Will the extinction of marriage be complete? Will people still believe it's possible to stay in a marriage "till death do us part"? Will the concepts of marital faithfulness and loyalty to a single person be relegated to museums and historical documentaries?

Here's a warning for those who have not yet woken up: forces in society are conspiring against marriage and the family, and these attacks are only getting stronger.

THE METAMORPHOSIS OF MARRIAGE

In general, the media (movies, TV, the Internet, books, newspapers), cultural norms, politics, laws, celebrities, the curriculum in schools and universities—in fact, all of society's major centers of influence—are becoming, or have already become, anti-marriage.

What does this mean?

- There will be a sizeable decrease in the number of marriages.
- Cohabitation will become more and more common—inferring that long-term, absolute commitment is impossible.
- Infidelity and affairs will increase (yes, even more) and become more and more tolerated.
- Casual encounters involving three people, with sex as the sole purpose, will become more acceptable.
- Men and women will become even more predatory.
- Women will view men as nonessential, and will grow even more independent.
- Women will bounce between no longer believing in love (or men) and the search for happiness at the expense of their own sense of worth.

Note: All of the above are ALREADY happening in today's society. It's the metamorphosis of marriage, and time will only continue to speed up this process.

You may not be able to change what's happening around the world, but within *your* own world, inside *your* marriage, you can and must. This is not a question of *whether or not* your relationship will come under attack, but rather *when*. The question is: will you know how to protect it from these attacks when they come—that is, if it's not already under attack?

MARRIAGE IN THE FACEBOOK ERA

New challenges, for example, such as the Internet, social networks, communication technologies such as SMS and MSN, the proliferation of pornography, an anti-marriage culture, easy divorces and the advancement of women in society are a few of the recent phenomena affecting couples in the twenty-first century, and many are not prepared to handle these new challenges. Couples today are faced with a new reality, a world that their parents never knew, in fact, no generation has ever known. Ask your grandmother how she would have known if her husband was having an affair, and she'll say, "lipstick stains on his shirt" or "another woman's perfume" and similar signs. Today, it is so much easier to have an affair behind your partner's back.

Mark Zuckerberg, the creator of Facebook, has been billed as one of the greatest destroyers of homes in Great Britain. According to a study published by Divorce-Online, a website that specializes in divorces, Facebook is cited as the reason for one in every three divorces in the country. Close to 1,700 of the 5,000 cases mentioned that inappropriate messages to the opposite sex and comments from ex-girlfriends on Facebook were the cause of their marital problems. In the U.S., the American Academy of Matrimonial Lawyers released an article stating that, in 2011, Facebook is cited in one of every five divorces.

To have a better idea of the seriousness of the situation, recently in Brazil a new exclusive social network was launched for married people who "live in a marriage without sex and want to find others in the same situation." Committed men and women are targeted by this site, which offers them a "discreet way to have an affair." In less than six months, the site already had more than three hundred thousand users in the country, making Brazil the second-highest in terms of number of users, outnumbered only by the United States, where the site had already existed for a number of years. The site offers a private email account and credit card charge without the name of the user appearing on the statement, all to facilitate casual sexual encounters, without ever leaving a trace for the betrayed spouse. Their slogan reads: "The true secret to a lasting marriage is infidelity."

Outrageous, right? You haven't seen anything yet.

What's the fastest growing business in the world, with greater profits than Google, Apple, Amazon, Netflix, eBay, Microsoft, and Yahoo put together? Porn. In 2006, the profits in this industry brought in US$97 billion. More porn movies are made throughout the world than any other category, by far. This translates to an average of about 37 movies per day, or more than 13,500 per year. Brazil is the second largest producer of these movies, only surpassed by the United States. One study reported that seven out of ten men aged 18 to 34 visit pornographic websites on the Internet. Women, once uncomfortable with this type of behavior, have been increasingly seeking out porn in order to please their partners. "But thank God we're Christians and this doesn't affect us." Don't be too fast to jump to conclusions. A survey of Christians in the U.S. revealed that 50% of men and 20% of women were addicted to pornography. Another survey held solely among pastors revealed that 54% of them had seen pornography within the last 12 months, and 30% within the 30 days preceding the survey. Is anyone immune?

MAN VS. WOMAN: THE FINAL BATTLE

For the first time in the history of the male species, men are feeling displaced and lost in their marriages. With the advancement of women in practically every facet of society, they have become competitors to men and moved on from the traditional role of helpers. Men—who used to be the sole hunters, providers, and protectors of the family—now view their role as divided and often taken over by women. Women have become hunters too.

Today, most women work and contribute to the family's income. In many cases, the wife earns more than her husband, a trend that is likely to increase, since university enrolment among women is higher than men.

What effect does this have on marriage? Here are a few examples: women have become more independent than men and are less tolerant of men's flaws. Wives are making decisions without their husbands' input, causing serious disagreement between them. In an attempt to please women, men have become more sensitive. Men have taken a backseat in their marriages. Husbands feel disrespected by their wives, and at times even useless. In other words, women have become more like men, and men have become more like women—a complete chaos and confusion of their roles.

But women are not only advancing and competing with men in the workplace. A study performed by the University of São Paulo revealed a disturbing statistic for married men. Extramarital affairs among women are growing at an alarming rate, and the younger they are, the more they cheat. Of the 8,200 women surveyed in ten cities throughout Brazil, only 22% of women over 70 years of age confessed to having had some kind of extramarital affair. The rate rises to 35% for women between 41 and 50 years of age and reaches a peak of 49.5% between 18 and 25 years of age. This means that half of all young married women today betray their husbands. As women have emerged from the simple stay-at-home-mother role to a more active role in society, college, the workplace, etc., this has made it easier for infidelity to proliferate.

Add to this the steady stream of conscious and subconscious attacks by the media leveled at the foundation of marriage: soap operas, movies, magazines, blogs, news, fashion, music, groups, and "ethnic" parties . . . Each one is a pointed gun firing round after round: why get married? A piece of paper isn't going to make a bit of difference . . . They get married, but they really aren't one in truth. If it doesn't work out, they get divorced and marry someone else . . . Both men and women do the same. There's no such thing as love, it's all an illusion . . . Marriage is a prison . . . How could anyone put up with the same person for twenty, thirty, or fifty years? Marriage is old-fashioned . . .

Every day, a new anti-marriage argument is created.

If you value your relationship and do not want to become just another statistic, bulletproofing your marriage is the key to its survival. It's time to defend and protect your most precious investment, before it's too late. Let's fight for this.

If you are genuinely committed to bulletproofing your relationship, then start to follow the advice and tasks that we recommend in this book.

TASK:

What are the greatest threats to your marriage right now? Identify these threats, so that you are aware of the areas of your marriage that need the most help.

(Wait! Before writing down your task below, ask yourself if you plan to lend out or give this book to someone when you've finished with it. I'm sure that you would not want them to read your notes or know all about the struggles you are facing in your marriage . . . In this case, we suggest that you write down your tasks somewhere else—a notebook, diary, or computer file. Do what you think is best. I simply wanted you to think about that before you started.)

 /BulletproofMarriage

On our Facebook page:
I've identified the current threats to my marriage. #BulletproofMarriage@ BulletproofMate

 @BulletproofMate

Tweet: *fb.com/ BulletproofMarriage post: I've identified the current threats to my marriage. #Bulletproofmarriage*

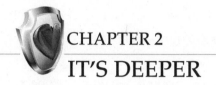

CHAPTER 2

IT'S DEEPER

If I were a fly on the wall of your living room or bedroom when you and your spouse were having an argument, what would I see? Perhaps a coldness when you speak, harsh words, an angry tone of voice, irritation, constant interruptions, accusations, criticisms, and so on. One day you disagree about the way to discipline your children, the next day about how your husband "friended" an ex-girlfriend on Facebook, and the following day you disagree about how your mother-in-law interferes in your marriage. The point is, the real problem is not always what you see. The problem goes much deeper.

A simple example is when a husband has an addiction. His wife sees him giving in to it and thinks that that is the problem. She gets angry, criticizes him, tries to talk to him and asks him to change, but nothing ever changes. Why not? Because the addiction is not the real problem. There is a root, something deeper, that is the cause of the addiction. She doesn't know what it is—perhaps neither does he—but the two of them will go around and around in circles arguing about what they see on the surface.

The visible problems are the leaves, branches, and trunk of the tree, but the true causes are less apparent and more difficult to detect and understand. And yet, the only reason for visible problems to exist is the fact that there is a root that feeds them. If there were no roots, the tree would not exist.

Once you've identified the root of the problems in your relationship, you will understand why you and your partner act the way you do. The arguments about the leaves and branches will diminish, as will the bad atmosphere that exists between the two of you. The elimination of just one bad root will result in the solution of several problems at once, and permanently! This is the power behind this shift of focus. Learning to focus your attention and energy on the real problem can transform your marriage, because everything, including our behavior, depends on how we look at things, what we look at, and how we interpret what we are looking at.

Stephen Covey talks about an event in his life that taught him the importance of putting this into practice.

He recounts how one day he was quietly riding the subway, calmly reading the newspaper. The subway car was not full. It was pretty quiet and various seats were available. At one of the stops, a father entered with two very mischievous children and sat down next to him. The boys started running around, were loud, and immediately brought an end to the peace everyone had been enjoying. The father was sitting with his eyes closed and seemed not to care about anything that was happening. Covey did not understand the father's indifference and angrily turned to him and asked why he was not doing anything to control his children. As if he had only then noticed what was happening, the father replied, "You're right, I'm sorry. We only now left the hospital. Their mother just passed away. I don't know what to do, and it seems like they don't either . . . "Covey apologized and began to comfort the man. Immediately, all the anger he had felt for the father and children disappeared and gave way to empathy.

But what caused Covey's previous angry attitude to change? He began to look at the situation in a different light. Before he was given that information from the father, Covey watched what was happening through the lens of his own principles and values. "How can a parent allow his children to be so out of control? If they were *my* children . . ." But after receiving this new information, his view of things changed radically. Notice how none of the people changed: the children did not stop misbehaving, and the father did not do anything to control them. Covey's perspective of the situation was the only thing that changed, and along with it, his attitude.

The same thing happens in marriage. You judge your partner, and demand that he change because you see him through the lens of your own experiences, values, and concepts. But all of this conflict occurs when we do not understand or pay attention to what is the real cause behind each particular situation. So one of the first steps we need to take to transform the present reality of our marriages has to do with our perspectives—how we look at things, what we look at, and how we interpret what we're looking at. The challenge is knowing where to look, because the root is not always easy to identify. Let me try to help you by using another analogy.

ONE FLESH, TWO SETS OF PROBLEMS

When two people get married, they each bring into the marriage their own sets of problems and personal issues. What you don't see on the wedding invitation are things like, "John Doe, porn addict, severely *bullied* as a kid, extremely insecure as a man, will marry Jane Doe, abused as a child, a walking time bomb, who's ready to do anything that gets her out of her parents' house."

Their past is not going to be printed on the wedding invitations— in fact, it will not be printed anywhere. And yet, no one gets married without dragging their own baggage into the relationship. For example, in the case of this couple, John and Jane, do you have any idea where this union is headed?

On your wedding day, you typically only know 10% to 20% of the person you are marrying, at best, and most of that is knowledge about his or her good side. That's because most of us do a good job of hiding our flaws when we are dating. I say "hide" not because we intentionally deceive the other person, but simply because it's the natural process of getting someone to fall in love with you. A part of the dating process is doing all you can to make a good impression on the other person. You always wear the best clothes, think before you speak, walk away when you have flatulence, go out to eat at nice restaurants . . . In fact, the typical restaurant scene illustrates this point extremely well.

He'll choose a restaurant you like, and you'll be seated at the table and order your food. In between admiring glances, there are a lot of compliments about your hair and clothes, and the two of you enjoy the moment to the fullest. In the end, he pays the bill without complaining, and you both leave happy.

After marriage, this scenario happens a mite diffently. Dinner will be at the kitchen table, with minimum or no decoration. He'll say something about how the potatoes are not the way he likes them. Then, for the very first time, you'll notice that he makes an annoying sound when he chews . . . apart from other noises that are accompanied by a not-so-pleasant odor. When you're finished, you notice that he doesn't even take his plate over to the sink, let alone offer to wash the dishes . . . This is when you ask yourself: "Why did I marry this thing?"

Welcome to marriage! This is the time you truly begin to get to know each other. And with this "new" knowledge comes problems.

This is why I encourage those who are dating to be transparent and open with respect to their personalities and backgrounds, in order to minimize surprises in the future. Don't allow yourself to be so charmed by your date as to assume that he or she only has a good side. Dating is when you should discover everything you can about the person you are about to marry. Things like their past, family, how they were brought up, what kind of relationship they had with their parents, etc.

Marriage is not the place or the time to be surprised by the other person. Nobody wants to find out from their husband's ex-girlfriend six months after they're married that he has a son. The honeymoon is not the time for a wife to explain that she has difficulty being intimate with her husband because she was abused as a child. The more you know about each other, the less chance there will be for unpleasant surprises.

We once counseled a young man who came to us who was determined to leave his wife just weeks after they were married. His reason for leaving was that during their honeymoon he discovered that his wife was not a virgin, as she had led him to believe. He felt betrayed by the fact that she had kept this a secret, and had difficulty overcoming the emotional pain of knowing she had been intimate with other men. What to some would seem petty, to him was reason enough to consider divorce. It was hard to convince him to forgive her and overcome his negative emotions. They stayed together, but their early years of marriage were marked by serious problems.

A person's bad past should not be an obstacle to getting married. Let whoever has no skeletons in the closet cast the first stone . . . But it's crucial that we be aware of how our past can affect our present and future.

Imagine the patience and understanding required of a husband whose wife was sexually abused as a child. In order to determine whether or not he's up to the task, he has to be aware of the whole picture.

When two people get married, their pasts join together. And their pasts will determine their behavior within the relationship. For this reason, you cannot look only at the person you are with today, even if you have already been married for years. You have to know who this person is and what their roots are—where she came from, who she is, what circumstances and people influenced her and made her into the person she is today—and everything that contributed to this. Only then will you be able to fully understand the situation and respond effectively.

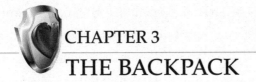

CHAPTER 3

THE BACKPACK

Imagine a bride and groom standing before a church altar. They are dressed for a wedding in front of all their guests. A pastor performs the ceremony. But attached to each of their backs, over her white gown and his rented tux, are large, heavy backpacks. Inside each backpack is their past, the baggage they bring into the marriage, whose contents they are about to discover: their upbringing, what they learned from their parents, past experiences, trauma, fear of rejection, insecurity, expectations . . . This is why anyone about to get married should behave like airport security: "Open your suitcase. I want to see what's inside!"

I've heard many couples say, "Your past doesn't matter to me. I only care about us and our future." Well, this may sound very romantic, but it will not stop either one of them from dragging their past into their present relationship. Your past is a part of you; it is impossible to get rid of. But you can learn how to deal with it, whatever it is. However, if you do not know each other's past, will you know what to do when it tries to interfere in the future, after you are married?

Let us share a personal example of how this baggage affects a couple right from the beginning.

5.6 SECONDS OF FREEDOM

When Cristiane and I got married, we began to have problems because I paid very little attention to her. Understandably, she became very demanding of me. Six days a week I would get up early and go to work, return late at night, tired, even bringing extra work with me to finish at home. On Saturday, what was supposed to be my day off, I would volunteer to go to work for at least part of the morning. Being young, I wanted to make an impression in my workplace, so I knew I would have to work hard at it.

I worked as if I were still single, forgetting that I now had a wife. I was unbalanced when it came to work and family. Cristiane stayed home most of the time, and when I came home at night, she would always ask me the same question: "How was your day?" The last thing I wanted to talk about at that point was how my day had gone, because I was exhausted. So I would give her a three-word answer: "It was good." Unsatisfied, she would insist: "Did anything interesting happen?" And I would answer with four more words: "No, it was normal." Obviously (but not so obvious to me back then), she felt excluded from my life. Not to mention, I only cared about getting some food, finishing the work I had brought home, and going straight to bed because I was dead tired. Add this all up, and what you have is the perfect recipe for an unhappy wife.

But that was during the week. On Saturday, things got worse. My dear wife thought, *Well, at least we'll be able to go somewhere on Saturday.* Poor thing. Since the most important workday of the week for me was Sunday, every single Saturday I was concerned about planning and preparing for the next day.

For the few hours that remained on Saturday afternoon and night, I just wanted to rest, but she wanted to go out to a movie. And because she had put up with my lack of attention throughout the week, she was even more determined on Saturday: "Where are we going today? Can we see a movie? Let's go out for lunch. Let's invite so-and-so to go out with us." And so I would look at her with "that face" and say: "Are you crazy? Don't you understand that this is the only time I have to be at home and rest?" I viewed her as extremely annoying and felt that she did not understand me at all. My defence was: "You knew what my work hours were before we got married. This is how it's always been, and now you're making it into a big deal." In reality, my days and work hours had not changed, but I had forgotten that while we were dating I would set aside time on Saturdays to go out with her. In reality, I was the one who had changed.

Cristiane Cardoso:

I was a pastor's daughter, and throughout my life I was either at home or in church. When I got married at seventeen, it was as if until then my right wrist had been handcuffed to my father's left wrist, and there at the altar, he had unlocked the handcuffs, put them on Renato's wrist, closed them again and given him the key.

By the clock, I had experienced 5.6 seconds of freedom . . . Of course, at the time it did not seem that way. I thought everything would change after marriage, because while we were dating Renato would constantly call me, and he would carve out one whole day of the week to spend together. He was super romantic, wrote me love letters all the time, and made me feel like the most important girl in the world.

However, my expectations went down the drain. Soon after we got married, Renato was transferred to New York, and I found myself far from my family and all of my friends. We lived an hour away from his job, which ate into even more of the little time we had together.

I wanted to follow my mother's example and be a good wife to Renato and make him very happy. I dedicated myself to our home, spent the whole day taking care of his clothes, cooked every day and always made sure to look good for him when he came home in the evening. But this was all very difficult because I was young and had just graduated from high school. The food I prepared did not taste very good, I would iron his linen shirts three different times, and even then, they didn't look right, the cleaning products burned my skin . . . and I thought, *Renato's coming home later, and he'll appreciate all my hard work*—Nope! He didn't even notice.

Renato was my first boyfriend and everything I had ever dreamed of, but I turned my marriage into a serious mess. I soon became sad and began to complain, cry, and be demanding. He would insist on saying that he had always been that way and that I should learn to live with it. I would have to adapt to this kind of life. The only days of the week that I got out of the house was when I went to church on Wednesday and Friday nights. Those were very special days of the week for me! No wonder I was so eager for him to come home all the other nights—he was the only friend I had to talk to. But he did not understand my needs and was never in the mood to talk. It even got to the point that I thought my husband was no longer in love with me.

I was so inexperienced and young, had never been in any other relationship, and so everything made me suspicious. At times I would arrive at church and see Renato counseling a woman (part of his job) and would get jealous. "How can he pay so much attention to people he doesn't even know and not care about me, his wife, who does everything for him. Does he know that I even exist?" After making comments like this, it would be all over—my husband would shut down even more. He would give me the famous "silent treatment" that would at times last for three days! He would speak to and smile at everyone else, but when it came to me . . . it was as if I did not exist. Obviously, that did not help me deal with all the insecurity I had brought into our marriage. It only made it worse.

My upbringing was very different from his. My family always spoke openly about what we were feeling, no matter what was going on. And so I continued to do the same at home with Renato, but instead of getting upset with me, saying what he had to say and then returning to normal, he simply wouldn't say anything, and then he'd look at me annoyed and stop talking to me for days. This contrast in dealing with problems made our disagreements even worse. On top of the problems at work—the pressure and responsibility—he would come home and have to face even more problems. Everything was new to me, and I had no one to talk to, and so I wanted him to be my friend, but all I got was a frustrated husband who thought I was a nag.

It was only when I stopped demanding his attention that I saw results. He began to do what I liked and what pleased me, without me even asking. Today we talk about everything; we are best friends and enjoy each other's company very much. But we were only able to do this after we learned how to deal with each other's baggage.

Renato Cardoso:

I noticed her jealousy, which upset me a lot, but I could not understand its root. I had no idea what was in her baggage. And so whenever she demanded something of me, forced me to do something or accused me of anything, I would simply shut her out. This was when she began learning a little more about the baggage I was carrying.

I grew up watching my father deal with his marriage problems by shutting my mother out. I saw this all through my childhood. When my mother did something that he did not like, my father would "punish" her with the silent treatment for two, three, or five days. The longest time, believe it or not, was eight months! If there were a silent treatment competition, my father would be the record holder . . .

I hated it when they were not talking to each other. My mother would try to make peace and do things to please him, but he would not let go of what had happened—little things that were often nonsense. This led to a horrible atmosphere for us four children. I always told myself that I would never be like that when I got married.

And yet, when I got married, I did exactly the same thing to Cristiane. In the end, experience is the better teacher than theory. I knew what I was doing was wrong, but that's what I had learned to do and what I had seen all through my childhood and adolescence. That was the heavy weight in my backpack.

EXCESS BAGGAGE

The truth is, we simply act out that which we have learned. I didn't have any other reference point than that. We end up repeating our parents' mistakes because their behavior (not their words) is our school. I did not want to act that way, but it seemed as if I was programmed to act like my father. Even though Cristiane would apologize to me, that was not enough to change my behavior.

In a relationship we have to unlearn the bad before we can learn the good. We have to identify our bad habits, what is not working, and eliminate them so that we can then develop new and better habits. This recognition is very painful, but of utmost importance if we are going to change.

As you can see, early on in our marriage Cristiane and I had a lot of problems because of the baggage we brought into our relationship. I was not a bad person, nor was she, but when we put our baggage together, the results were bad. This happens in all relationships. Every single person is lugging around baggage, their set of principles, values, experiences, culture, worldview, beliefs, habits, their past, traumas, family/school/friends' influences, dreams, and much more.When two people come together in marriage, most of their problems come from things in their baggage that cause conflict. Because of this, it is crucial that you get to know the other person on a deep level and discover their roots, so that you understand why they behave the way they do. It is also crucial that you know and understand yourself, because this will help you develop ways of dealing with your own roots and, in turn, resolve any differences and conflict.

This is what happened with Cristiane and me. Years later, I became aware of our baggage and began to understand why we behaved the way we did. Her baggage was the expectation of a perfect family, which she came from, the image of a perfect father, the insecurities of never having a boyfriend (on the other hand, I had recently broken off an engagement), a childhood and adolescence with zero leisure time or social life. This explains why Cristiane expected so much of me, was jealous of women I had no interest in, demanded so much of my attention, and couldn't wait to get out of the house and do something with me.

OPPOSITES ATTRACT, AND THEN CLASH

What's interesting is that her baggage clashed head on with mine, which is normal for most couples. Opposites attract, but once they're married, they clash and drive each other crazy.

My family was very different from hers. I had three brothers and one sister. We did not treat my poor sister, how can I put this, very gently. We were rude. My mother was constantly caring for my father and us kids, and rarely demanded anything for herself. She lived for her husband and children. My father . . . well, I've already told you what he was like. With this as my background, I found Cristiane to be a little boring, highly demanding, clingy, and always complaining about something—a real nag at times. I had the image of a strong woman who could handle anything engraved in my mind because of my mother, and this did not help the way I viewed my wife, which explains my cold-shoulder and harsh treatment toward Cristiane.

Another part of my baggage: I grew up surrounded by women. I had a sister, many female cousins, many aunts, female friends in the neighborhood, at school, in church, and girlfriends here and there. I didn't see any difference between female and male friends. After marriage, this did not help the root of Cristiane's insecurities, which explains her jealousy.

At home, we were always a hardworking family. My father got up every day at five in the morning, even on Sunday. He put my older brother and me to work at the age of twelve. Hard work has always been in our blood. When I started working in the church, before I got married, this attitude got stronger, because now I was not simply working for money but to help others. Because I had married a pastor's daughter, I assumed she would totally understand the devotion I had toward my job. But in reality, I drove Cristiane crazy. She did not understand me, and I did not understand her. For many years we tried to change each other, without success.

When and how did we finally overcome our differences? Only when we began to understand what was behind our behavior and made adjustments to deal with the root of each conflict.

I finally understood that her problem of jealousy and suspicion was my responsibility as well. I could not make her change, but I could reduce the triggers that I caused that were feeding her insecurities. I realized I could help boost her confidence in herself, and in me. I stopped debating and blaming her for her jealousy and gave up my friendships with other women, reducing my interaction with them to the bare minimum. I backed away from them and used every opportunity to communicate to Christiane that she was the only woman in my life. My goal became: reassure my wife.

ATTENTION FROM THE OPPOSITE SEX

By the way, many couples find it difficult to make a decision concerning this. They are unwilling to give up those friendships that are putting a strain on their marriage. As a general rule, I learned that it is not wise for a married man to have close female friends, nor should a woman have close male friends. Having close friends of the opposite sex is playing with fire. It's common for people to resist the idea that this is wrong, because the truth is, we like the attention. We also believe that as long as we have no intention of betraying our spouse or getting involved with the other person, then nothing is wrong. We are far too confident in ourselves, and we tend to forget that we are not in control of our, or the other person's, feelings. So please understand: no friendship is more valuable than your marriage. Instead of holding on to close friends of the opposite sex, learn to become your partner's best friend.

Cristiane Cardoso:

I had already learned this lesson firsthand in school from experience. At one point I got tired of my friendships with other girls because of all the gossip back and forth, so I started hanging out with guys instead of girls. On one hand, it was good because they respected me and didn't talk about everyone else's lives. On the other hand, some of them started looking at me in a different way, and I didn't even know it. When I realized that some of them had crushes on me, I had to distance myself and told myself I would never be friends with boys again . . .

When I got married and saw Renato with female friends, it drove me crazy! I was afraid he would develop feelings for them the same way my friends at school had for me. In the beginning, I would constantly demand he explain himself about every relationship, condemning him for them. I ended up using any weapon possible to distance him from those friendships.

It was not easy to overcome those insecurities, but I did. But what helped me the most with that challenge was to focus on what I was doing wrong, instead of focusing on him.

At times, a woman is right, but the way she goes about solving her marriage problems is wrong, which puts even more stress on the relationship. When I began to change my attitude and focus more on myself, I was transformed into a more pleasant wife and Renato stopped tuning me out.

The great thing about this is that whenever we invest in ourselves, we begin to see what we are doing wrong. For example, I discovered that I also had a calling, and that this calling was not about helping my husband timidly in the background but actively, right alongside him. I began to overcome my own weaknesses, especially my shyness. My life no longer revolved around him. I took my place at his side, and we had a common goal: to work for God.

Women do not always realize that whenever they get clingy, they push men away. Husbands will rarely put up with a direct attack from their wives. When Cristiane changed her behavior toward me, she became more desirable. Soon I was more interested in her, felt closer to her, and started asking her to go out with me.

This is when I was inspired to balance my time between work and marriage. I began to pay more attention to my wife because I knew she needed it. Overall, when we both understood the roots of our behavior and did what was necessary to deal with them, the problems came to an end.

A HAPPY MARRIAGE TAKES WORK

Men are often workaholics, but we have to understand that marriage is also like a job, a business. If you do not work on your marriage, it will eventually go bankrupt.

Happy marriages don't just happen, they take work. When you see a happy couple who have been together for many years, understand that it is not due to luck. It is not because they "were made for each other" or because they are "a perfect match." If we were to take a closer look, we would notice that they are constantly working on their marriage. After twenty-two years of marriage, Cristiane and I continue to work on our relationship. Carelessness, being lazy about taking care of something, or forgetting important things are enough to create minor problems. That is why we never neglect this.

Unfortunately, many couples give up right from their wedding day. They act as if they no longer need to make an effort to win each other over as soon as they return from their honeymoon. Okay, we're married! Job done.

Men, in particular, tend to do this. For us, the period from the first conversation up to the honeymoon is the most interesting for our competitive nature. It's exciting to know that she's willing to go out with us, that she's hooked and thinks we're awesome . . . It's sort of like a game for men. (Women, I'm just being honest . . . this is our nature. You will get a better understanding of this later on in the book.) And so, our wedding day is like a trophy presentation ceremony.

When a winner receives a trophy, he puts it on the shelf, and it becomes part of his past. This is what many men do with their wives after marriage. We think the game is over, that the hard work of conquering her has finally come to an end. We've even got a piece of paper to prove it—our marriage license!

Let me give you a friendly word of caution: the game has only just begun! If we stop working on our marriage, we will lose the game . . .

TASK:

What are the main items in your and your partner's baggage—the things that have affected or may affect your relationship in the future? Take a few minutes to think about the major events that have marked your lives, or that formed your character, principles, and values—what determine your behavior. This task requires a trip into the past, careful meditation, and most probably a conversation with your partner to find out what his/her answers are. Write down what you are able to identify, but feel free to come back and add more things to this list as you discover them.

/BulletproofMarriage

On our Facebook page
fb.com/BulletproofMarriage
post: *I have started to go through our baggage.*
#Bulletproofmarriage

@BulletproofMate

Tweet: *I have started to go through our baggage.*
#BulletproofMarriage
@BulletproofMate

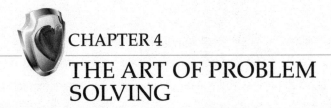

CHAPTER 4

THE ART OF PROBLEM SOLVING

Baggage, personality differences, tastes, expectations . . . all this and more set the stage for the problems that creep up in a relationship. When they appear, and you do not know how to handle these differences, they remain unresolved and the marriage will deteriorate. If nothing changes, within a few years divorce will take place. What is divorce, if not an exit strategy for marital problems that the couple never managed to resolve?

Couples who once loved each other end up separated or living together as strangers in the same house because they are unable to resolve the conflicts in their relationship. Instead, they insist on trying to change each other. They think: *If I can make my husband/wife more like me, then our problems will be solved.* Then they criticize, accuse, point out each other's shortcomings, all the while defending and justifying their own actions. They run around in circles and never get anywhere. When one of them finally gets tired of the insanity, he or she decides to separate.

Being happily married is an art—the art of problem solving. There are at least seven billion problems in the world today—every human being has at least one, and most probably many more. Yet, we are all still here, and alive, in spite of our problems. We manage to solve some problems, and others we learn to live with until we hopefully find the solution. Problems are a part of life. Those who are the most skilled at problem solving are the most successful; those who are the least skilled are often the least successful. It is no different in a marriage. If you want to bulletproof your marriage, you have to first decide to become an expert problem solver.

But note: problem solving is not about changing people. Our focus must be to resolve the conflict between us and change the situation, not fight the other person. It is a mistake to think that we can change another person and tailor him or her to our liking. Not only will we be unable to accomplish this, we will end up viewing the other person as the problem and reach the conclusion that we have to leave him or her and find someone else. This means that if we do not learn to solve problems in our first marriage, we will go into our second marriage without this skill and discover the same problems or different ones and continue to experience an unsuccessful marriage. Is it a surprise that divorce rates for couples that get married for the second, third, or fourth time continue to rise?

Our method is more effective: we want to help you to identify the real problems, discover their roots, then eliminate and prevent them from returning.

One fact that intrigued us the most was when we discovered that there is practically no difference between the divorce rates of Christians and non-religious people. A belief in God, the Author of marriage, does not seem to be enough to prevent people from getting divorced. This is interesting, because if there is one group that should be skilled at keeping their marriages together, it should be those who believe in God. But why doesn't this happen? Because most of these people cannot, or do not know how to, apply their theoretical knowledge about love to their relationships on a daily basis. For example, it's one thing to know that God is love, and a completely different thing to know what to do, for example, when the person I love lies to me. A person's Christianity truly starts to be challenged when he or she enters into marriage.

MIRROR, MIRROR ON THE WALL

Marriage serves as a mirror. As you were getting ready this morning, you looked in the mirror at least five times (if you're a woman, more like twenty . . .). Why do we look in the mirror whenever we get the chance? Because our eyes are unable to give us a clear picture of how we appear to those around us. If there were no mirrors, no cameras, or camcorders, we would never know what our faces looked like, or some of our other body parts, or what we looked like from behind (though some of us would not find this a bad idea). But thanks to mirrors, we can look at true reflections of ourselves, and even see those areas that are hidden from our own eyes.

The same holds true in marriage. Our spouse is our mirror because he or she is a true reflection of who we are—our good side as well as our bad side. When you look in the mirror, you like certain aspects of your body and dislike others. When you put on a nice outfit, you look in the mirror and think to yourself: *I look good in this! These shoes match this belt perfectly* . . . But there are certain things that you do not like to look at. If you think your nose is crooked or too big, or that the gap between your teeth is too big or your hips too wide, you feel bad whenever you see them. I know someone who positions her head at a 45-degree angle toward the camera whenever a picture is taken because she thinks her head is too big . . . and like her, everyone deals with what the mirror shows them the best way they know how! But one thing is certain, it does no good to swear at or fight with your mirror. It's not its fault. It is simply showing you the truth.

When you place yourself in front of the marriage mirror, you begin to discover flaws that you were unaware of. After I got married, my bad temper was revealed to me. I had not noticed this problem before, because as a single man I had never had to live as close to anyone in the role of a husband. When we were dating, we were close, but not as close as after we got married. The closer we are to the mirror, the clearer and sharper our image. This is what happens to all couples.

The problem is that up to the wedding day, all we hear from the other person is how wonderful we are. "You're so beautiful." "I love your honesty." "You make me feel so good, I forget all about my problems." You only hear praise. So you start to think: *This person's going to make me really happy. I'm going to marry her.* We expect to continue to hear only good things about ourselves after we get married. But the mirror does not lie. Once we're married, we are now closer to our mirror, and the other person begins to reveal our flaws to us . . . Rather than taking advantage of this opportunity and changing, we start to project our own flaws onto the other person and point out what they need to change: "He's so annoying!" "She's so spoiled, she cries about everything." "I don't want to act like that, but you set me off." In other words, we blame the mirror.

It's only natural to get defensive when our flaws are being pointed out to us. Nobody likes that. But that's not a smart attitude to have. If you decide to ignore the mirror because it's always showing you things you dislike about yourself, you'll never improve in any area. Instead of defending your actions and attitudes to your spouse, use their *feedback* positively. Take advantage of that information to improve.

As long as I saw Cristiane's pointing out my flaws as a source of irritation, I did not become a better husband, or a better person. But when I used my reason, I began to see that my wife was providing me with a personal challenge to improve, so I started using her as a mirror to deal with my flaws. You can do this too.

So please understand this from the very beginning: *you cannot change another person. People only change when they decide to change.* For that reason, whenever someone tries to force us to change, our natural reaction is to resist. It's a way of protecting our own identity, our right to be who we are, even when it doesn't please others. I know this sounds crazy, but this is how humans behave.

"So is there hope for me?"—you might ask yourself. "Are you saying my husband will never change?" "Is my wife always going to act like this?" I'm not saying that he or she will never change. I am saying that it's not going to be you who is going to make them change. But there's good news: you can influence and inspire another person to change. That's why you are reading this book, so you can learn to do this.

Everything starts with a focus on yourself, instead of pointing the finger at your partner's mistakes. Just think: if you solve your own personal issues, half of your marriage problems will be taken care of— even before your partner changes one bit.

When you change and stop demanding that your partner change, you will be taking the first step to inspiring change in him or her, without demanding anything. Instead, look at yourself and admit your own mistakes. Open up your baggage and remove anything that's weighing you down. Don't worry about his or her baggage for now. First, focus on understanding yourself, so that later on you'll be able to understand your partner better.

You might have started reading this book because you're only interested in discovering techniques to change your husband or wife. But the truth is, you're going to learn how to change yourself. If you embark on this mission of becoming a better person, your marriage will improve, and this includes your spouse. But if your mission is to change your spouse, you should stop right now. We will not be able to help you. Nobody can.

CEASEFIRE!

If you really are determined to bulletproof your marriage, then begin to follow the advice and tasks that we are going to suggest to you in this book.

The first task is to declare a *ceasefire*!

When two countries are at war and want to seek out a way to end that war, the first step is declaring a ceasefire so that a peace agreement can be negotiated. They stop shooting at each other as a sign of good faith.

If you have attacked your partner in any way, even sporadically, you should immediately stop. Here are some examples of what I mean: sarcastic comments, accusations, verbal attacks, bringing up past mistakes and the like. But there are also passive forms of attack such as: the silent treatment, "forgetting" important information, treating your spouse with indifference, staying out late, and so forth.

Think: how can you make your relationship bulletproof to external attacks, when you insist on making internal attacks? This is not wise. The external attacks that we're forced to go through are already plenty to deal with; we don't need to turn each other into enemies. Our enemies are the problems we're going through, not each other.

Therefore, if your relationship is at war, stop right away! Declare a ceasefire. From this point on, as you read this book, be civil to your partner and treat them with respect. This will give you a chance to breathe, gather your thoughts, and learn new ways to solve your marriage problems.

One more reason to declare a ceasefire: avoid sabotaging your own efforts at bulletproofing your relationship. Think: if you continue to attack your partner as you read this book, your problems will only grow. There will come a time when you look at this book on your nightstand and say something like: "It's no use! I'm not going to read that stupid book anymore"—followed by the thought of shoving this book down your spouse's throat . . . Not a good idea!

This is your new task to bulletproof your marriage: Ceasefire!

TASK:

Use the space below (or somewhere else if you do not want to write in this book) to list the ways you normally attack your partner. Think of all the ways that you attack, from the least to the greatest, and include them all.

_____

_____

_____

_____

I promise to stop treating my partner like this and to start treating him or her with respect, self-control, and consideration.

 /BulletproofMarriage

On our Facebook page
fb.com/BulletproofMarriage
post: *I am starting the "ceasefire" today.*
#Bulletproofmarriage

 @BulletproofMate

Tweet: *I am starting the "ceasefire" today.*
#BulletproofMarriage
@BulletproofMate

PART II
EMOTION VS. REASON

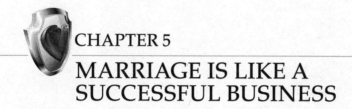

CHAPTER 5

MARRIAGE IS LIKE A SUCCESSFUL BUSINESS

Having a happy marriage is an art—the art of problem solving. Those with better problem-solving skills will be more successful in their marriages. Those with poor problem-solving skills will experience more failure in their marriages. If you want to bulletproof your marriage, you have to begin by making the decision to become an expert problem-solver.

Problems are normally avoided, ignored, or postponed rather than resolved in a relationship. The cycle typically goes like this: a couple has a disagreement, they debate over the issue without much progress, tempers flare, one ends up hurting the other with words or with their inflexible attitude, both get tired of arguing without getting anywhere, they give up out of exhaustion and frustration, then time goes by until the same disagreement comes back again.

The seven-stage cycle of unresolved problems in a marriage.

In this cycle, nothing gets resolved. The problem is postponed or temporarily fixed, but it always comes back. And when it does, it's almost always worse. Many couples think that time will solve their problems. "Let's give it some time" is an expression that many use when they don't want to deal with a problem when it first appears. But marriage problems are not anything like wine. They never get better with time. When it comes to conflict in a relationship, putting it off will always make it worse. In this case, time is a couple's enemy.

One of the main reasons why people put off dealing with marriage problems is that they're normally extremely painful experiences. A lack of good communication skills, verbal attacks, and anger cause couples to avoid the issue rather than face it. This is especially true for men. Many men run away from serious conversations with their wife because they're unable to hold a conversation on the same level. Women, on the other hand, become frustrated because it seems that they can never get their husband to understand them.

But it doesn't need to be this way. There is an effective way for men and women to solve their marriage problems and prevent them from coming back, without hurting anyone in the process. I call this method: treating your marriage like a business.

THE OBJECTIVES OF A BUSINESS

Why would a person start his own business? What's the goal? There could be many. Earning more money would be an obvious goal. The independence of being your own boss would be another. Many feel the need to live up to their full potential and see a business as their means of accomplishing that. Others want to make a difference in the world they live in; they want to help others. One thing is certain: every company has at least one goal. No company exists just to exist. Everyone's searching for results, and those results become the focus of everyone in that company—especially the owners. If there are no results, there is no reason for the company to exist.

Marriage is also a business. No one gets married without a goal or wanting to see results. When a bride and groom think about marriage, they are actually thinking about goals, about making their dreams come true, such as: starting a family, having children, making your partner happy and being happy yourself, living with the person you love for the rest of your life and feeling loved, building a financial future together, having someone by your side in your struggle to make your dreams come true, enjoying great physical intimacy, finding a true friend in your partner, etc.

Cristiane:

Though Renato and I had the same goals when we got married, I also had some expectations that did not match his. And it was exactly where we had differences, where we were not aligned, that we had problems. It's so important for couples to know each other's expectations for marriage. If we had sat down to talk about this before getting married, we would have known what to expect from each other.

At times, couples even talk about their goals, but with the passing of time, expectations begin to outweigh the initial objectives. If they don't make adjustments and remind themselves of their goals, frustration will cause them to attack each other: "You always said this or that, but now you're trying to change things." Instead of dancing to the music, they each begin to dance to different music, and that's where things get complicated.

We recently organizedThe Love Walk through our TV program The Love School all over Brazil as well as around the world. About 10,000 people came together with one objective: learning more about your partner through dialogue. This idea developed out of an experience we had a few years ago, when Renato invited me to a park to talk.

We had been married for more than fifteen years, but this was the first time we spoke our minds freely and expressed our desires and hopes in one conversation. He learned about my dreams, my worries, my problems, what I wanted and did not want, and vice versa. These were precious hours that greatly strengthened our marriage. After that conversation, I knew exactly what he expected of me. I knew what to do to support him and how to do it.

Many times we think we're at our partner's side, when in fact we're far away because of our ignorance of what we both really want from each other.

A marriage also has goals and must produce results, just like a business.

Why is it important for you to understand this parallel?

A company's goals guide its day-to-day activities. The decisions they make, whom they hire, how they train their employees, the products they make and their advertising—everything is designed around the goals and results that the company wants to achieve.

When we applied this concept to marriage, we found that most couples unfortunately do not have this same train of thought. They're caught up in their busy lives, and they get lost in emotion and quickly lose sight of why they got married in the first place. Once their goals are forgotten, the decisions they make and the things they do no longer contribute to the happiness and success of the marriage.

When a husband gets involved with a lover, for example, he has clearly lost sight of his marriage goals. But this is not just taking place at the moment of his affair. It began the very instant he decided to look at another woman and allow himself to be interested in her. That look caused him to wander off the path that would lead to the goals for his marriage. He lost focus and abandoned his company's goals. His persistence down this path will inevitably lead his marriage into bankruptcy.

If one spouse enters into the marriage with the thought that it might not last "till death do us part"—that person will end up doing things that will ruin the marriage and bring it to an end. If on the other hand, when a person sees himself by his partner's side till death, then he will do all he can to keep that relationship going. In other words, our focus on the goal determines our behavior.

In the beginning of my marriage, whenever I had a misunderstanding with Cristiane, my goal was to win the argument. I wanted to prove that she was wrong and I was right. And because I'm a better debater than she is, I would almost always win. What a short-sighted goal. I would win the argument but lose my wife's intimacy and friendship. This is what many couples do: they would rather be right than happy.

When I learned that my marriage is like a business, I realized that even the smallest decisions and actions must be linked to our long-term goals. Today, whenever we argue, which is seldom, I always ask myself: what outcome do I want from this conversation? My goals come to mind, and I make sure the conversation goes in the direction that will achieve those goals.

HOW DO COMPANIES SOLVE PROBLEMS?

Do you think Steve Jobs ran into problems when he started Apple? Of course he did. From Apple to the hotdog stand around the corner, every business starts with dreams and goals, then immediately encounters problems—and not just in the beginning. No matter how successful a company might be, it must address and resolve issues on a daily basis. The survival of any business depends on their problem solving. If problems are not resolved, the company will go bankrupt. In fact, if you are an employee, this is the real reason you were hired: to solve problems. (And you thought it was because they liked your resume!)

No matter how many employees a company has—only two, 2,000, or 20,000—successful businesses achieve their goals by solving their problems. But the interesting thing is, there is no loving relationship between employees. Often, it's the exact opposite. We hardly ever hear an employee say, "I love my boss!", nor do we hear of one co-worker writing love letters to another co-worker in accounting. Now, if they can succeed under these circumstances, they must be doing something right that brings about good results.

Question: *Why do couples with a relatively small amount of problems, who love each other dearly, often fail to overcome the challenges in the marriage relationship?*

Answer: because they use the wrong tool to solve problems: emotion. The secret behind successful businesses is that they avoid using emotion in problem solving and use reason instead. They understand that nothing can be solved with emotion. The workplace is a zone for intelligence and action, not a zone for emotion or this or that feeling. For that reason, they achieve their goals regardless of their employees' feelings, and regardless of whether one employee dislikes another. In those kinds of companies, you learn to separate work and interpersonal relationships, and never mix the two. They reason: "I don't like my boss, but he told me to do this, and he pays my salary. So I'll do what needs to be done." This means: they separate emotion from action, people from work, and focus on the desired outcome. They use reason, not emotion. Keep this phrase in mind:

Emotions are the wrong tool for solving problems.

Think back: every time you made a decision based on emotion, you ran into trouble. Anyone who runs his business by emotion ends up failing. Have you ever heard the saying: "Never mix business and friendship"? This sums up the motto of many successful entrepreneurs. "I don't care who you are, whether or not I like you or you like me. What matters is that we have this problem, and we need to come up with a solution in order to achieve our goals. What are we going to do to solve this?"

This is what businesses focus on: what are we going to do?

What can we do to increase sales? What are we going to do to reduce spending? What are we going to do to surpass our competitors?

Do. Do. Do. Not feel, feel, feel.

Feelings are not the tool to solve problems.

A DISCOVERY IN THE LABORATORY

We have a section in our program The Love School called "The Laboratory." It involves taping a couple as they argue about the problems in their relationship. Afterward, Cristiane and I watch the couple, identify the problems in their communication and behavior, and then give them suggestions on how to improve. Before we turn on the cameras, we place the couple alone in the studio, sitting and facing each other, and we ask them to start talking about anything they think needs to be resolved between them. Then we turn on the cameras. It's a real experience . . . As a result, we call it "The Laboratory."

One of the discoveries we made while watching these couples was a pattern of intense emotion during the conversation and a lack of focus on solving the problem. Driven by feelings of frustration, anger, sorrow, contempt, and misunderstanding, couples tend to spend most of their time going over their list of "Who's Worse." It goes something like this:

Wife: You're so messy. You leave things scattered all over the place.

Husband: The problem is you want things done right away. If I don't put my shoes away the minute I take them off, or put my plate in the sink, you immediately start yelling at me.

Wife: You're so inconsiderate. Can't you see that I've just finished cleaning the entire house? The least you could do is not make a mess. You know I like things to be organized.

Husband: You're not all that organized. The other day I opened your desk drawer and it was a mess. What's up with that? So the desktop is organized, but the drawers are a mess. That makes no sense!

Wife: Okay, but if you'd help more around the house, you'd know how I feel!

Husband: So I never help?

And this goes on and on and on. Ten, twenty, thirty minutes later, and they're still going, jumping from one problem to the next. Note that their conversation never focuses on the problem or on what they should do to solve it. Because of emotions, one person is trying to prove to the other that they're not that bad, or that the other person is not as perfect as they might think they are. In the end, it's the pot calling the kettle black.

The Who's Worse List

Pot: "You're black!"	Kettle: "No, you're black!"
Messy	Wants things right away
Disorganized	Yells
Inconsiderate	Is not that organised
Doesn't help around the house	Doesn't appreciate help he gives

By the time the conversation ends, the list is usually quite long, balanced, and both egos are wounded. Of course, nothing is ever resolved. No wonder many couples have given up talking to each other. Why talk? Why listen to the one you love go through his or her list of all your flaws? No thanks. I'd rather watch TV.

But, if they used reason instead of emotion, they would focus on the problem and how to solve it. At the end of the conversation, they would have reached a conclusion and would both know exactly what to do to avoid that problem next time. And . . . no one would end up feeling hurt.

Now imagine, what would it be like if employees acted like the couple above when it came to solving their company's problems? The company president would call the VP of sales manager into his office and say:

President: John, our sales are dropping.

John: Well, why don't you get up from that comfortable chair of yours and come help us? Maybe sales would't be so low, then.

Of course, the conversation would never reach the emotional level of the couple above because it would end pretty fast with, "John, you're fired. Please pick up your paperwork from HR." Because John doesn't want to be fired and his boss doesn't want to lose a good manager, they would instead focus on coming up with a strategy to improve sales. They would use intelligence and reason, not emotions or feelings—even though their emotions are very real and present.

Emotions are the wrong tool to solve problems—at work and also in marriage. How I feel about a problem does not matter. What matters is what I'm prepared to do about the problem.

No one "feels" the solution to a problem. John does not walk up to his boss and say, "Leave it to me. I feel that sales are about to improve." If he did, he would also be sent to HR . . . Solutions are found by thought, reasoning, coming to a conclusion, and acting upon that conclusion—never by following an emotion.

By using reason, not emotion, to solve problems, companies with tens, hundreds, even thousands of employees stay focused on one goal—and they don't even love one another. Surely, a couple who love each other and use their intelligence should be able to benefit from this tool, stay together, and solve their problems.

TWO RULES FOR BUSINESS SURVIVAL

Every business, every company, has to follow two basic rules to survive. If you break just one of these rules, you will lose your job or your business. What are these rules?

1. Identify, solve, and prevent— Identify the problem (understand what it really is, and what causes it), solve it, and if possible, prevent it from reoccurring. This is the basic rule for a successful company. For example: several customers have complained about long delays in product delivery. The company has to find out what is causing these delays, solve the problem, and implement standards and methods that will eliminate the chance for these delays to reoccur.

2. Don't take anything personally—In business, reason must be used. If you're emotional and take things personally, you will not be effective and will usually not last very long on your job. Your personal life, what you feel about what's going on at home, or with your colleagues, does not matter to the company. You have to learn to separate things. The focus of the company is its goals and what needs to be done to achieve those goals. Your boss expects you to be an adult, not a spoiled child who throws tantrums whenever something doesn't go according to plan.

Focusing on the problem and setting emotions to the side—this is how businesses survive and thrive. By using the same tools, your marriage can also overcome all challenges.

CHAPTER 6

TEN STEPS TO PROBLEM SOLVING

The two basic rules described in the previous chapter enable successful companies to thrive and advance on a daily basis by solving not only small, easy problems, but large, complex ones as well.

We can divide the art of problem solving into ten distinct steps, which can also be easily adapted to the institution of marriage. Any person who is successful at his job, whether boss or employee, already follows these ten steps, though most do not think of them in such a structured way. A focus on results and an emphasis on reason rather than emotion lead them to follow this natural process of problem solving.

An entrepreneurial mind is trained to follow this process without much thought, much like how the muscles in our legs are used to going up and down stairs with hardly a visual clue from our eyes. But since emotions play a big role in our marriages, they tend to overshadow our mental abilities, making what is clear and logical at work not so clear and logical at home. Because of this, we will break down this process to help you understand how it can be applied to different situations in marriage.

We are going to compare two typical problems in business and marriage. This way you will understand how these same steps we use to solve problems at work can also be used to solve problems in your marriage.

Suppose you are the manager of the Human Resources department of a company named Gadgets Ltd. (It's just an example. It was the first name that popped into my mind.) You are responsible for all the the details of managing the company's employees. A problem is brought to your attention: there has been a high turnover in the company's receptionist position. Over the past three months, four receptionists were hired and then quit. The company is now looking for a fifth receptionist. The high cost of hiring and training, a drop in employee morale, and the lack of consistency in the office are just a few of the negative effects. It is your responsibility to solve this problem. Your boss wants results.

Meanwhile, at your company Marriage Ltd., you are also facing a problem: a husband wants more physical intimacy, and she thinks they enjoy more than enough already. This is what has been affecting the couple's mood off and on, causing him to be upset with her and causing her to feel pressured by him. Both want to settle this standoff.

Let's look at the ten steps to solving these problems:

1. Call a meeting and immediately talk about the problem

At the company: The first thing you should do is call a meeting of the people involved and start a communication with them to find out what is really happening. I want to emphasise the word "immediately." That is to say, you cannot wait to deal with the issue, because an overlooked problem will only continue to grow. In the business world, quick responses are a big advantage over the competition. Therefore, you cannot waste time. Immediately hold a meeting with everyone who might have useful information about the situation: the hiring manager, supervisor, front desk manager, etc. You should do this regardless of how anyone is feeling about the issue. What has to be done must be done.

In the marriage: Here is where most couples start making mistakes. Most often when problems start to surface, both tend to go their separate ways and brush aside any thoughts of resolving the conflict. They think that by postponing the discussion, they'll fix the problem. Men are generally more guilty of this, but it varies according to the type of problem that needs to be resolved. Women are usually the ones to point out a problem. They bring up the issue in the hope that their husbands will join them in searching for a solution. Men tend to be more simplistic, less concerned about details, and have little patience when it comes to discussing things they do not consider a problem. In an effort to keep his anger under control and steer clear of an argument, he avoids talking about the problem, tries to delay the conversation, or quickly finds a way around it. He comes up with excuses for why he cannot listen to his wife: "Not now, I'm tired, let's talk about it tomorrow." (Men sometimes do this in the hope that their wives will forget about it and leave them alone. We really are naïve!)

When a problem surfaces in marriage, you should take immediate action to solve it. Remember, problems are not like wine; they don't get better with time. Therefore, get together as quickly as possible to communicate and expose the problem. Eventually, it will need to be solved, so the sooner the better. If we wait till later, it might get bigger. So, act fast.

In this case, or any other one, the couple should get together as soon as possible and expose the problem that they are facing in bed. Regardless of how they feel, feelings don't solve problems. What matters is that there is a conflict, and your company cannot prosper when there are unresolved conflicts. Therefore, the best time to solve the problem, with few exceptions, is now.

2. Listen

At the company: Step number two. After meeting with your team, you should listen to everyone involved (your hiring manager, HR supervisor, front desk manager, etc.) to find out why the receptionists are quitting. You want to listen to them because you're a professional, intelligent boss. One of the worst kinds of bosses is the know-it-all. Have you ever worked for someone like that? When he or she is made aware of a problem, they walk straight up to their employees with an order and a pre-fabricated solution: "From now on, you are going to do things like this." They don't care to listen to anyone, because, of course, they know everything and employees are just employees. But you cannot be like that. The best insights to a problem come from those who are directly involved with it. So, you want—you need—to listen to them carefully. Begin the meeting by talking less and listening more.

In the marriage: This second step usually starts off wrong for couples with marital problems, and that's because of emotions. One of them initiates the conversation by pointing out the other's problem, and the other immediately gets offended and defensive.

Remember the Who's Worse List that couples make in The Laboratory? This is where they go wrong. Instead of carefully listening to each other, they grow defensive until they get tired and give up on the conversation. While one partner is speaking, the other stops listening and uses that time to formulate his or her next answer or retaliation. They have stopped listening to each other. There is a natural psychological explanation for why this happens. When we feel that we're being attacked, our fight or flight instinct is switched on. This is such a basic instinct that it can be seen in any animal. If you attack a dog, for example, his instinct of self-defence and survival will either cause him to attack back or run away. Humans use this same instinct for everything. So what does this mean? Whoever initiates a conversation has the power to determine their partner's reaction—positive or negative. A conversation that begins in an accusatory or critical tone will provoke a fight or flight reaction to the conversation. Ideally, the problem should be presented in a way that is not directed at any one person. For example, if a husband says, "You're a cold person, you never want to do anything with me"—his wife will feel that she's being attacked and will be tempted to answer: "You're an animal. All you care about is sex." The war is now on! Now, neither one will listen to the other; all they will do is attack or defend their position. But if he begins the conversation by saying, "Honey, is there something I can do to make our sex life more satisfying for you?"— her reaction will be different. Did you notice the difference? The way a conversation starts determines whether or not the listener is willing to participate.

When your spouse begins to expose a problem, resist the temptation to defend or justify yourself. Initially, just listen and gather all the information. Allow him to freely express himself. Do not assume that you already know what the problem is, because the other person may have a different view of what it really is. So be smart: listen.

3. Ask

At the company: To identify and understand the root of a problem, you need to ask questions that will provide you this information. Do we know why each of the four receptionists quit? How were they recruited? Who hired them and what criteria were used in the hiring process? What was their salary? How does that match up with comparable positions in other companies? What's the job description for this position? How far along are we in recruiting the next secretary? In other words, you need to ask the necessary questions for a better understanding of the problem—and continue listening attentively to the answers. Notice how these questions are not accusatory, nor are they looking for someone to blame—they're simply aimed at gathering relevant information.

A technique developed by Japanese professionals states that if you define a problem and ask why it is happening at least five times, you're likely to discover the root of the problem. For example:

- The house is cold. (Problem) Why is that?
- Because the heating system is broken. And why is that?
- It hasn't received the proper maintenance. Why not?
- Because I didn't want to pay for it. Why not?
- Because I'm too stingy and don't like spending money unless I really have to. (Root of the problem!)

The immediate solution to the problem of the cold house is, of course, to fix the heating system. The permanent solution, however, is a change in that person's mind-set about money. He needs to readjust his thoughts and understand the fundamental concept of "spend now and save later." If he does periodic maintenance on the heating system, he will spend some money now, but not as much as he would when the system breaks down due to a lack of regular maintenance.

Of course, he can decide to fix the heater now and not worry about the root problem. In that case, he needs to understand that the problem will come back in the future . . . Asking "why" in an intelligent manner is a good way to discover the root of your problems and find a permanent solution.

In the marriage: Asking your spouse questions when he or she brings up a problem that needs solving is a great way to not only understand the situation, but to show that you are listening and that you're interested in understanding the other person. It's the same thing you would do at your job—focus your questions on discovering the root of the problem. Are you satisfied with the physical intimacy in our marriage? What makes you feel that way? What do I do that you like or dislike? Does intimacy play an important role in our marriage? Why is that? How do I make you feel pressured? When do you find sex pleasurable? When is it not pleasurable? Is there a time of day or night that you prefer to spend time together? Which time of the day or night do you not like it? How often do you think we should be intimate—what is a healthy amount of intimacy? These questions will help you explore what is behind the problem, and will certainly shed light on other questions. Again, notice how the questions do not have an accusatory tone and are focused on discovering the cause of the problem without attacking anyone.

4. Focus on the facts

At the company: In business, we work with facts, figures, data, and evidence. Of course, intuition, experience, personality, principles, and other more abstract inputs influence our decisions. However, our basic and most reliable decisions are those that are tangible, solid, real, and indisputable. Because of this, your thoughts about the receptionist desk at Gadgets Ltd. are mainly based on verifiable facts, rather than assumption or mere opinion. If someone from accounting says, "I did not like the last receptionist"—this is not an important fact. The solid information that the HR manager hands you is much more important: "The last four receptionists claimed they were leaving because they found better paying jobs elsewhere." That is a fact. "Other departments routinely give the receptionist extra work, and she ends up not being able to do her job, or the extra jobs"—says the reception manager. This is another fact.

In the marriage: Here's a typical scenario at Marriage Ltd.: The husband comes home from work and leaves his shoes, socks, and other things all around the house, which his wife has spent all day cleaning and organizing. He rolls around on the living room floor with the dog, and in five minutes he's messed up what she took hours to clean. Exasperated, his wife comes in and says, "Could you not be such a slob?" Even though she's being honest about the way she feels, she has not stated a fact. I've never come across a husband who works out an evil plan against his wife on his way home from work every day: "I hope the house is nice and clean because then I can make a big mess of it. Ha, ha, ha . . ." The fact is: he's not a complete slob. This is how it may seem, what she may feel, but the facts are: "He leaves his clothes all over the place when he gets home from work, and he seems to value being home and relaxing after a hard day's work more than he does a neat and clean house." For now, whether he's right or wrong is not the issue, but rather the obvious facts that can be seen by anyone looking at this scenario, not just his wife.

We must be careful not to have a spirit of judgment toward our spouses. In fact, if we really wanted to be a judge, the first thing we would have to learn is to focus only on the facts, the evidence. A good judge ignores his feelings and looks at the facts, nothing else. And yet, we frequently judge our spouses, and end up being bad judges because we always rule in our favor . . .

Focusing on the facts is another way to separate emotion and personal feelings from reason and the problem.

In the case of a couple who have a problem in the bedroom, the observable facts may include, for example: they were only intimate twice during the past month, even though the husband asked his wife about it ten different times, and each time she said "no." Maybe she feels pain during intercourse. Maybe the wall between their bedroom and their child's room provides little privacy. She may confess that sex is a low priority for her in the marriage and that she misses the friendship they had in the beginning. She might also add that she feels used by him when he pressures her to be intimate when she doesn't want to be.

Facts are facts. They are verifiable bits of information that can be observed by anyone. They are not opinion. This step leads to effective conversations and clears the way for a solution to be reached.

5. Explore ideas

At the company: Notice how up till now, throughout the first four steps, you have only gathered information that enables you to understand and define the problem. Now you're ready to begin exploring possible solutions. In the corporate world this is known as *brainstorming*—an open group discussion aimed at generating ideas and ways of solving a given problem. Everyone is invited to contribute ideas, the more the better, until the best ideas are identified, and the best proposal is chosen.

Maybe your HR manager will suggest increasing the receptionist's salary so that it matches what other receptionists are getting paid in the marketplace. Someone else may come up with the idea of paying more than the going rate, while at the same time increasing the receptionist's responsibilities. Another might suggest that a job description be written and clearly explained to the next receptionist, and that other company departments be made aware of what she is, and is not, allowed to do. The receptionist manager might come up with the idea of offering a career plan as an incentive for her to remain with the company, showing her the opportunity to grow in the company. All ideas should be accepted and given fair consideration.

In the marriage: This democratic process of sharing suggestions and ideas is extremely important in a marriage. Many spouses sin by wanting to impose their solution on their partner. A good leader knows how to involve his co-workers and employees in the search for solutions— not just for political gain, but because he knows that two heads are better than one. In the same way, a couple should search for a solution that best solves their problem, rather than pushing their own agenda.

Looking at the problem, which should now be defined after the first four steps, the couple should at this point ask themselves: how can we solve this problem and prevent it from happening again?

This stage is marked by its creativity and amount of ideas. The couple should feel free to share ideas without fear of being criticized, condemned, or ridiculed. After all, there's always more than one way to solve a problem. The wife may suggest: "Maybe you could try to spend more time with me like we used to do in the beginning. I feel closer to you when you do that. I know I have to be more understanding of your needs as well, and shouldn't push you away all the time. I am going to work at being more intimate with you because I know how important it is. If you could do something about our bedroom wall, I think I'd be more up for it. Privacy is very important to me."

He could also give other suggestions: "Let's see a doctor about the pain you're feeling during intercourse. I admit that I say things I shouldn't when I get angry. I'll be more careful with my mouth. What can we do to balance out our needs so that no one feels imposed upon? I want to make your enjoyment a priority, so can you let me know what feels good to you? I'm going to learn more about this and get some professional help."

It's possible that neither of them has the ideal solution. That's when one idea would be to get professional help, someone who could steer them to an answer.

6. Propose a solution

At the company: From all the ideas that were suggested, you have to choose the most realistic and effective one to resolve the problem for now. If a permanent solution cannot be found, then choose one that should at least last for a very long time. After all that's been heard, let's say that you and your team arrive at the following proposal: match the salary that other receptionists are paid, draw up a career plan for her within the company, and meet with the new receptionist once a week for the first three months to identify any possible signs of job dissatisfaction, with a plan to seek out a solution in time, thus minimizing the possibility of losing another receptionist. This proposal is chosen because it appears to deal with the main causes of the problem.

In a marriage: When trying to come up with a proposal for a solution, keep in mind that the best answer to any marriage problem is always the win-win solution. If one loses, both lose. So remember the company's goals, the team, not just the individuals. In the same way a company would handle it, propose the solution that addresses the cause of the problem.

The couple reaches an agreement, for example, to seek outside help from a doctor who is a good source with expertise on how to help increase a woman's sexual pleasure; the two of them decide to put more effort into fulfilling their spouse's sexual expectations with a balance—yielding to the other's needs when and where it's necessary—without making each other feel imposed upon. They will also insulate their bedroom wall.

7. Agree on a plan of action

At the company: Now that you have a proposal, everyone needs to believe in it and its feasibility. It can't be implemented unless those in charge are in total agreement. The question to be answered is: does everyone believe in and agree that the proposal will solve the problem? Everyone involved needs to believe in and support the proposal.

In the marriage: If having the support of everyone involved is absolutely essential in the workplace, it is doubly important when it comes to marriage. But you do not need to agree on everything. Sometimes you will have to "agree to disagree." When this happens, start looking for some common ground.

Take short steps. Many problems cannot be solved right away, and you may have to repeat this process many times. But do not allow disagreements over some points hold you back from taking action in another area where you're already in agreement. This step must end with both of you saying: I agree that if we did this, we can solve the problem.

8. Define who will do what, and do it

At the company: Who will do what, how, and when? In successful companies, no one leaves a meeting without reaching a decision on these three points. Tasks must be defined and distributed to those responsible, so that everyone knows their role with respect to solving the problem. With the solution proposed in the previous step, as the HR Manager, you must seek the board's approval to increase the receptionist's salary. The person responsible for training and staff development will prepare a possible career path for the receptionist within the company. The front desk manager will remain in contact with the new receptionist on a weekly basis to detect any problem. Deadlines are agreed upon.

In the marriage: She will make an appointment with the doctor, and he will go with her; he will look for a good book that explains how he can be more sensitive to his wife's sexual needs. He will stop pressuring her, and they will both be more careful about using harsh words. He will hire someone to install soundproofing in the bedroom wall; he will be patient with her, and she will be more attentive to his needs. Of course, the "doing" is the most important part in all of this. Once again, you have to ignore your feelings, your own will, and simply do what is right and necessary to solve the problem. Just like in a business, the directors might not feel like paying the receptionist a higher salary, but if that will help avoid spending more on continually training new people for that position, then it must be done.

9. See if it works

At the company and in the marriage: Though a lot progress has already been made, the problem is still not solved. Up till now, all we've done is talk about the problem! And so, both at the company and in a marriage, after everyone has reached an agreement and has been given a sufficient amount of time to execute the plan of action, the results need to be analyzed. Don't abandon the process during the eighth step, which is where most people are tempted to assume that they've solved the problem. Carefully track the proposed solution step by step and make sure it's working.

At the company, a good result would be that the newly hired receptionist becomes a long-term employee and moves up in the company.

In a marriage, the couple should start enjoying a significantly healthier sex life, should be less frustrated, and notice a change in their mood, which will help draw them closer to each other.

10. Yes? Continue. No? Repeat the process.

At the company and in the marriage: By following these ten steps, you will likely solve the problem, if not completely, at least partially. If your problem is not completely solved, don't get discouraged. That is absolutely normal. More than one attempt may be necessary. The truth is, this process will never end, because new problems pop up every single day in a business and at home, and we have no choice but to become experts in implementing these steps as we move forward.

I often hear people say, "I've tried everything. My husband is hopeless." "My wife is never going to change. I've done everything you can possibly imagine for her, but she hasn't changed." Wait a minute. Let's take a closer look at what you just said. *I've tried everything? I've done everything you can possibly imagine?* I don't think so. You may have tried three, five, ten different ways to solve the problem, but don't say that you've tried everything. There is always something different that you haven't yet tried. *"I've tried everything"* is an emotional phrase. Reason, on the other hand, refuses to accept the idea that there is no solution to a problem.

Therefore, refuse to give up when the problem is still there after the first attempt to solve it. Repeat the ten steps, except this time you know what did not work the first time around. This is what we do at work all the time.

THE 10 STEPS

1. Meet and open communication inmediately	*Uncover the problem*
2. Listen	
3. Ask questions	
4. Focus on the facts	
5. Explore ideas	*Seeking solutions*
6. Prpose a solution	
7. Agree to a plan of action	
8. Define who will do what, and then do it	*Executing the agreement*
9. See if it's working	
10. Yes? Keep at it. No? Repeat the process	

If you take a close look at these ten steps, you'll notice how there is a complete lack of emotion in them. They are a logical and rational process, not an emotional one.

The beauty of this process lies in the fact that you already practise this at your job every day. (Nobody could run a business or hold on to a job without it.) You instinctively follow these ten steps already, though you might not think of them as ten distinct steps. Even so, you apply them several times a day, every day. You probably don't even need to *memorise* these ten steps, because you already know them by heart. You just need to *transfer* this knowledge to your marriage and apply it when you have to solve a problem.

THE TELEPHONE TEST

Whenever I suggest this idea of treating your marriage like a successful business, many people respond bluntly, saying it'll never work for them. They say, "I put up with people on my job because I don't have to sleep with them. I am not romantically involved, so it's easier." However, if we take a deeper look, it becomes obvious that this is completely wrong.

Let's be honest: the real reason we control our emotions at work has nothing to do with whether or not we like the people we work with—it has to do with money. You don't swear at your boss or get into a shouting match with a fellow employee because it would cost you money. This is why every once in a while we see people explode at work at someone—they no longer care about their jobs and are already planning to leave. So, the truth is that we control our emotions because we have the extra motivation of not wanting to lose money. Now, answer this question: what about finding the motivation to control our emotions because we don't want to lose our marriages?

This brings us to another benefit of viewing your marriage like a business: seeing marriage as your biggest investment. Married couples tend to be more stable financially and in every other area of their lives, such as health, faith in God, and family. It makes no sense to sacrifice your emotions to succeed at work, but not in marriage. What good is a successful career when you are not successful in love? What good are an abundance of material possessions when you have no family to share them with?

Let me paint a common scenario for you. A husband and wife are at home arguing about something, exchanging insults back and forth. Tempers flare. All of a sudden the phone rings. One of them checks who's calling, realizes it's an important call, and decides to answer. However, before he does, he gives an order to his wife in an angry tone: ZIP IT FOR A MOMENT, I HAVE TO ANSWER THIS PHONE

CALL! He answers the call, and lo and behold, his voice has changed in a nanosecond. In a friendly, respectful tone, he says: "Hello? Hi, there, how's everything? Sure, go ahead, I have time to talk . . ." The person on the other end of the call would never imagine that two seconds ago this same person was screaming in rage! In other words, we do have the power to control our emotions in the middle of an argument with our spouses!

TASK:

Let's put the ten steps into practice. Identify a problem that still has not been resolved between the two of you. It may be better to avoid anything too serious, for now, until you gain more confidence and control over your emotions. Think of an issue that's not too sensitive, but needs to be resolved. Start by identifying the problem. Write the problem down in one or two sentences. Then, sit down and go over this problem with your spouse and make sure there are no distractions so you can resolve this matter.

 /BulletproofMarriage

On our Facebook page
fb.com/BulletproofMarriage
post: *I started using the 10 Steps to Problem Solving. #Bulletproofmarriage*

 @BulletproofMate

Tweet: *I started using the 10 Steps to Problem Solving. #BulletproofMarriage @BulletproofMate*

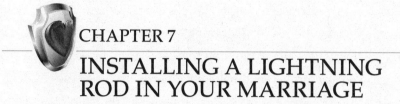

CHAPTER 7

INSTALLING A LIGHTNING ROD IN YOUR MARRIAGE

As the construction of tall buildings increased in popularity in the eighteenth century, the risk of them being struck by lightning also increazed. People realised that the higher the building, the greater the risk of it being hit by lightning. This problem caused numerous fires and deaths, yet no one had a remedy or even understood why lightning was attracted to certain buildings.

The overly religious, who had no true knowledge of the subject, said that lightning bolts were "arrows of judgment from God" or that they were the work of demons. And yet, curiously, churches were the buildings struck most often by lightning because of their high steeples. The bell-ringer was usually the first victim . . . The problem was so serious that authorities began to warn people to look for shelter during storms "anywhere but inside or near a church." No one understood why, but according to the religious, the Almighty was targeting His own churches or allowing Satan to do so—not to mention that nobody went to church on a rainy day . . .

The actual reason for this had nothing to do with God or the devil. In 1752, Benjamin Franklin discovered that lightning carried electricity. Based on this finding, he invented the lightning rod—a metal rod that, when fixed to the top of a building and connected to the ground by a metal wire, would absorb the electric charge and redirect it into the ground, thereby freeing the building and its occupants from danger. God was thankful, and the devil laughed at the overly religious, who were left feeling rather embarrassed.

Emotion is a form of energy, like electricity. When tempers flare between a couple, the risk of "lightning" increases. If emotions are not controlled, they will result in outbursts that can lead to the destruction of a marriage. And like certain buildings were more likely to be struck by lightning, certain people have short fuses and are more difficult to get along with because they allow themselves to be contolled by their emotions.

And yet, having a short fuse is not a good excuse; neither is blaming God or the devil for your negative emotions. We are all affected by emotions, and we are all given the intelligence to control them.

We are not encouraging you to repress your emotions. Nobody's a robot. Marriage is one of the greatest tests of our temperament, and it's unreasonable to think that we can simply keep stuffing our negative feelings inside and not suffer some sort of negative effect. Sooner or later, you will explode.

Instead of repressing your emotions, you should find somewhere else to redirect them other than at your partner. Benjamin Franklin discovered that lightning was a normal occurrence, but that it was possible to redirect it to a place where it would cause no harm. In the same way, we need to install a lightning rod in our marriage so that we can discharge our emotions elsewhere. But how can that be done?

BEFORE THE LIGHTNING ROD

In the beginning of our marriage, we had no lightning rod. Sparks flew whenever tempers flared between Cristiane and me. Her lightning bolts were a demanding, insistent, and jealous nature with harsh words added on. Mine were the cold shoulder and the infamous "silent treatment" I would give her.

Whenever my emotions flared, I didn't know how to handle them. Since I have a calm nature, I'm normally a quiet person who tends to stuff my negative feelings inside. And so I would not explode, I would implode. Because I didn't want to fight with Cristiane, I refrained myself. However, inside I would think about all I wanted to say to her, would imagine a conversation between us, but I would keep everything to myself. (If I could have expressed just 10% of the conversations I had in my head, I would have solved the problems so much faster . . . Later, as I counseled other couples, I discovered that I was not crazy. I was not the only one who did this!) I was repressing my emotions. The lightning bolts were burning me up inside, and my anger was causing Cristiane to burn as well.

And so, I would stay angry with her for days and give her the silent treatment. At times, after stuffing a lot of negative emotions inside, I would explode and behave like a psychotic horse trapped in a burning stable. Can you picture that? Not a pretty sight.

There is no way to avoid having emotions. After all, we are made of flesh and blood. But we must also remember and believe that we are intelligent beings, not animals that simply follow their instincts. If on one hand we are influenced by emotions; on the other hand, we can make our emotions submit themselves to our intelligence.

That is what I learned and began to put into practice in my marriage. These days, there are almost no situations where Cristiane and I provoke each other's temper. But the few times where friction or frustration does occur, my lightning rod is to ask myself: "What's my goal in this situation? What end result do I want to achieve by solving this issue?"

So I remind myself: "I don't want to be angry at her . . . I want to go to sleep tonight with my arms wrapped around her . . . Resolve the problem in a way that's good for both of us . . . I don't want to be upset and walk around the house giving her the silent treatment for the next two or three days, etc."

When I focus on these goals, I end up using my emotions as the energy to solve the problem rationally. I use my mind to redirect my feelings and emotions, and then focus on the results I want to achieve. This process helps me control what I feel rather than letting my feelings control me.

Once I put my mind in control of my emotions, I begin the process of resolving the problem with Cristiane. At this point, lightning bolts no longer exist. My reason automatically redirects them toward my goals, instead of Cristiane. Of course, this requires that I take a few minutes to collect my thoughts. If you have a similar problem, you will also have to learn to resist the impulse to engage in combat and not allow your emotions to control your mouth.

The message is: find a way to vent your emotions at something other than your spouse. What I wrote about above is what works for me, but you have to find what will work for you. For example, Cristiane has a completely different, but very effective, lightning rod.

Cristiane:

Whenever I get angry about something, I can't do what Renato does without praying first. So my lightning rod is prayer. I go into my room, or somewhere private, and unload my anger on God—not against Him, but as a way of venting my feelings. I have found that prayer is a channel through which I can take any frustration to God. After all, He is the Almighty, and can handle a woman's fury . . . unlike my husband. When I started to put this into practice, God made me see that every time I insisted on a particular thing and butted heads with Renato, I was not pleasing to Him. And so, when I pray, I not only unload my emotions on God, but I also gain the strength to make the right decision and resist the temptation to turn that issue into a big deal. I give myself a cease-and-desist order and refuse to create a storm in a teacup, because that storm will only attract more emotional lightning bolts . . . So, I decide to offer up my emotions as a sacrifice.

By means of prayer, I stopped demanding things of my husband and started demanding answers from God; I stopped mistrusting my husband and began to trust in God; I stopped using harsh words with my husband and started speaking openly with God. This has been my lightning rod ever since. It works, and I suggest that every couple use this method as well, especially women.

Women tend to be more emotional and less rational. This is why prayer is a great way to take back control of our emotions and begin acting more rationally. If you've never tried it, make a sincere effort.

I'm not encouraging religious prayers and rituals. What I am encouraging is honest conversations that we could never have with anyone else—not with a husband, father, mother, or friend—because they wouldn't understand. But God, who made us and knows exactly what's going on inside, understands, and gives us the strength to act wisely.

The best thing about this is that we're taking our issue straight to God. We're going straight to the Source. If we are unable to change or force our partners to understand, God can. There are things that only God can do, things that we often label as unsolvable.

I remember a particular instance where I was right and he was wrong, but it was no use because he refused to admit it. The more I tried to explain, the more critical and upset he became. The "poor me, this is unfair" feeling came over me, but I made the decision to stop butting heads with him and go take a shower. In the shower, I had a serious conversation with God: "Lord, you know who's right and who's wrong in this situation. You know what really happened. So you have to be the one to clear this up because there's nothing else I can do. I don't want to get angry with Renato. I don't want to do to him what he's doing to me. I want you to give me justice." When I stepped out of the shower, Renato still had that face of "I'm going to be upset with you for days." I didn't say one more word. I just went to sleep, trusting that God would sooner or later give me justice. The very first thing the next morning, Renato gave me a great big hug and asked me to forgive him.

STIRRING UP ANXIETY

When our emotions are not redirected at something that can wisely absorb and make use of them, we will either unload them on our spouses or suppress them. But when emotions are suppressed, they cause anxiety, which is emotion at its extreme. Anxiety is a sense of constant worry, nervousness, restlessness, and discomfort, caused by the uncertainty of what will happen next. Every human being deals with this.

This is one reason why God created prayer, so that we could pour out our cares on Him. If we do, He promises to take care of us.[2] This care includes freeing us from emotional burdens and showing us how to deal with our particular situation.

You can be sure that faith is not just something religious. Rather, it is extremely reasonable and intelligent. Once you learn to use your faith wisely, you can use your faith to solve your everyday problems.

You can be sure that there will be cloudy days, heavy rains, and storms in your marriage. And when they come, they will bring emotional lightning bolts. This is inevitable. But you can install a lightning rod in your marriage to redirect that emotional energy into something other than your partner. For some, a lightning rod may be counting to ten, others might prefer prayer, and still others may find that going for a walk works for them. In the end, you have to identify your own and determine whether or not it works for you.

And never forget: emotions are the wrong tool to solve problems.

---

[2] 1 Peter 5:7.

TASK:

What will you use as your lightning rod? Determine what it is and start putting it into practice right away.

/BulletproofMarriage

On our Facebook page
fb.com/BulletproofMarriage
post: *I have installed a lightning rod in my marriage. #Bulletproofmarriage*

@BulletproofMate

Tweet: *I have installed a lightning rod in my marriage. #BulletproofMarriage @BulletproofMate*

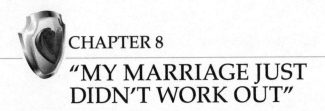

CHAPTER 8

"MY MARRIAGE JUST DIDN'T WORK OUT"

"My husband is great when he's not at home. He treats people well and everyone loves him. But when we're alone, he acts like the devil," a woman vented to us during a counseling session. Her words echo those of many husbands and wives who are frustrated by the two-faced behavior of their spouse. This two-faced syndrome is actually caused by a person's failure to correctly process their negative emotions.

When we fail to unload our emotions in a useful and positive way, they accumulate and we end up venting them all at our partner. We manage to hold our emotions in check in at work because we feel that strangers should not have to put up with our frustrations. Yet we wrongly conclude that our spouses are obligated to listen and understand, no matter how we behave. This is why we show our worst side to our partners—demonstrating much less care than we do for strangers. We are well-mannered when it comes to strangers, and a pain in the neck at home.

Obviously, this attitude causes a lot of wear and tear on a relationship. Deep wounds are created, and for that reason, many couples grows distant and their love begins to cool.

Understand one thing: the person you are at home is who you really are.

People who suffer from the two-face syndrome tend to make their situation worse when they note the following: their partner is always unhappy and complaining about their behavior at home, but when they're among friends and colleagues, everyone looks up to and admires them (because they don't know their other side). The conclusion they reach is: "My partner is the problem. Everybody likes me, but he or she doesn't. I have to get out of this marriage."

And yet, the problem is clearly not their partner. If they gave their partner the same courtesy and respect that they give to strangers, they would have their admiration and respect in return.

The person we are at home is who we really are. And so, even if this person divorces the partner who he thinks is the problem and gets married to someone else who seems to be wonderful and admires him greatly, this new person will eventually see his other side and have the same complaints as the first partner. The truth is we are the one with the problem. Many can't see this and go through life marrying this and that person, in an attempt to find "the right one." But the problem is not that we haven't found the right person, but rather that *we are not behaving properly at home*. We behave in a rational way with outsiders, and in an emotional way when we're at home, projecting our negative emotions onto our partner.

This is why so many succeed at work and are complete failures when it comes to love.

I MARRIED THE WRONG PERSON

When a relationship starts to go wrong and people's partners don't change—refusing to put up with their emotional trash and with their every whim—the "obvious" conclusion they reach is: "I married the wrong person."

"The marriage didn't go as planned," or "I married the wrong person," or "It turns out we're not soul mates" are expressions that exempt us from blame when a relationship fails. What happened to a sense of responsibility?

In the past, failed marriages were a personal embarrassment. When a couple had problems and complained to family or friends, the advice they were invariably given was: go back, talk things over, and fix it. The message was clear: fight for your marriage. If the marriage fails, you fail.

Today, advice-givers routinely take sides and say, "How dare he do that to you? You deserve better. Kick him out!" "I wouldn't put up with her if I were you. Remember, there's lots of fish in the sea. If this wife doesn't work out, find another one!"

All these phrases carry the same message: if things don't work out, marriage is the problem, or the other person is to blame—he's not the "right" person. The new trend is to blame the other person and take no personal responsibility for the failure of the marriage. It's as if marriage were a person with a will of its own that can be held responsible for the success or failure of a relationship, or as if the other person could guarantee a happy marriage all by himself.

The truth is, both are at fault. Marriage is not a person. The two people involved in a marriage are responsible for its success or failure.

THE SOUL MATE MYTH

One idea that has helped people sidestep responsibility for the success or failure of a marriage is the soul mate myth. The idea is that we all have a soul mate, someone who completes us and will make us perfectly happy. But where did this idea come from? It came from Greek mythology.

The story goes like this: humans originally had four arms, four legs, and a head with two faces. Zeus, the "almighty" Greek god, feared mankind's power and split them in half, condemning them to a life spent searching for their other half, the half that would complete them.

Since then, most cultures have come up with a romantic concept that everyone has a soul mate, someone who shares a deep bond with you, who is naturally affectionate, caring, loving, and sexually and spiritually matched. The implication is that they are the two halves of one soul, and they have to meet to be truly happy.

The line of reasoning for this myth goes on to imply that if the person I marry does not "complete" me, make me happy, understand me, and make me feel as good as when I'm eating chocolate, then he's not my soul mate. As a result, it would be useless to continue the relationship and try to make it work with the *wrong* person. The answer is to separate and continue searching for your soul mate—the *right* person.

This story may sound ridiculous and unbelievable, but I am convinced that this myth is deeply rooted in most people's minds. Performing arts are saturated with it, from Hollywood to reality TV, children's movies and romance novels. Everyone has seen the typical movie scene where a bride enters the church on her wedding day, catches a glance of the groom at the altar, and is overcome by doubt because she knows he's not her "other half"? And as we watch the movie, we're all led to believe that her soul mate is among the crowd of guests (or at the airport and about to board an airplane, depending on the movie you saw), and we're on the edge of our seats, hoping she doesn't make the mistake of marrying the wrong person. Then suddenly, she turns around and runs away, leaving the poor guy at the altar and is reunited with her "other half."

This has even infiltrated Christian circles, though there's no biblical precedent that God has created a soul mate for everyone, and so many people spend their lives praying to find their "other half" . . . And many remain single longer than they should because they're never sure whether this or that person is the one, and they haven't yet felt the "chemistry" with anyone. Some are even terrified by the idea of marriage. Doubt and fear are always present: "I am not sure if he or she is the right one."

The soul mate myth has gained popularity across a wide range of cultures and religions because the idea is romantic and attractive. The idea that only one person in the universe can complete you, and that God created you for that one single person, is beautiful. (But nobody stops to think: what if this person lives in Kazakhstan?)

It is not hard to understand what makes this idea so irresistible. It frees us from any responsibility of making it work on our part or from blame when the marriage fails. "It turns out he wasn't my soul mate." That's it. It's not your fault. You just haven't found your other-half . . .

People don't want to work at it; they want things to come easy. It's human nature. Microwaves, instant coffee, diet pills . . . Happiness at the snap of a finger.

Based on this train of thought, people act on emotion and not reason. Whenever they're faced with chronic problems in a relationship, they seriously consider throwing in the towel. "I tried, but it just didn't work out." "It's too hard. I don't think I'm going to make it."

Yet, what do we do at work when we fail to resolve a problem? Obviously, we try again. And if we fail a second time? We keep on trying different things until we find the answer because the company is counting on us, and this is how we make a living. We don't give up. We don't blame others. We take responsibility for our work and search for an answer. We brush our feelings to the side and use intelligence, creativity, and persistence in solving the problem. And if we're unable to come up with an answer, we make sure it doesn't affect the rest of the company. We do whatever it takes. We never give up. Never.

It's more than that, though. A persistent spirit, tackling a problem without fear, and finding an answer at all cost, this is the key to success in work and business. Successful people do not run from problems—they face them. They know there's something to gain from every challenge; every problem presents an opportunity. They face difficulties with ease, and gain more trust, which in turn affords them greater responsibilities at work and greater promotions.

When you earn a reputation for solving problems at work, everybody comes to you. You're the "go-to" person. Everyone knows that if they want something done, they need to give it to you. This gives you greater experience and respect and guarantees that you will grow as a person and in rank within the company.

On the other hand, when you don't take it upon yourself to solve problems at work, always make excuses, and blame others, no one wants to deal with you. Nobody wants to hear excuses. You were not hired to make excuses, to point the finger at other people or to complain.

Cristiane challenged me to become a better person. I had to learn to solve problems that I had never faced before. I also had to own up to my mistakes and be humble enough to change. I persisted, but change did not come quickly. I had to give it several tries and continually resist the thought of quitting.

This is what we have to do in marriage. What you're learning in this book are things that work. They have the power to transform your relationship and you as a person. But don't expect immediate change, because it takes time for fruit to appear. This is a long-term investment—especially when you're fighting to save your marriage all by yourself, and your partner is set in his or her ways or even skeptical about your changes. Don't expect your partner to believe you've changed when you started acting differently only yesterday. You have to win over their trust. Be consistent. The other person needs to see that your change is real and permanent. Accept this challenge—for your marriage and for yourself.

THE RIGHT PERSON VS. THE RIGHT ATTITUDE

The key to a happy marriage is not finding the right person; *it's doing the right things.*

If you do what is right for your relationship, your marriage will work. If you do what is wrong, everything else will go wrong.

When God created man and woman, He did not create them to be "soul mates." He first created man, then God decided to create a *helper*[3] for man, so that she could help him. He didn't say anything about one completing the other, nor did He make one responsible for the other's happiness. He simply said *helper.* A couple should see themselves as helpers, and be committed to helping each other. When this partnership exists, the couple will be happy and the two will become one, *one flesh.*

> *Therefore a man shall leave his father and mother and be joined to his wife, and they shall become one flesh.*[4]

Notice that the two only become one flesh after they have been joined to each other. They were not "two halves" before they got married, as if they were already predestined to become one for each other. This miracle happens when both are united in the one purpose of making their marriage work, no matter what happens.

Obviously, if you're still single and considering marriage, look for the best possible person. (Please don't marry a psychopath and assume, "My love can change him.") The fact is, a happy marriage depends less on choosing the "right" person, and more on the two of you doing the right things.

Following certain laws of co-existence is what makes a relationship work. When God created man and woman, he established laws to

---

[3] Genesis 2:18.
[4] Genesis 2:24.

 100

govern their relationship. If you respect these laws, you'll be happy. If you don't, there's not a soul mate in the world who will want to put up with you and stick around.

Laws work like this: obey them and they'll protect you. Disobey them and they'll punish you. If you jump off a ten-story building, you're going to die. The law of gravity will make sure of that. If you go on a safari and get out of the car to take a photograph next to a lion, you'll probably end up becoming his lunch. The law of the jungle guarantees that. Whether or not you believe in these laws, you are bound by them.

God's relationship laws are not a mystery. Things like forgiveness, treating others the way you want to be treated, patience, serving, helping, listening, being unselfish, honesty, faithfulness, respect, assuming the best, removing the plank from our own eye before you complain about the speck in your neighbor's eye, caring, etc., are the basic necessities for forming a relationship. People know they need to do these things, but many don't. Instead, they break these laws and reap the consequences.

If you obey relationship laws, they'll protect you; if you disobey them, they'll punish you. It's as simple as that.

This is the only path. People may try to place blame on the institution of marriage, make divorces easier, invent new types of relationships, spend their lives searching for a soul mate—but the only way for a relationship to succeed is for a couple to respect the laws that govern it. This power is in your hands. It's your responsibility. Understanding these concepts was the turning point in my marriage—and it started with a phone call.

CHAPTER 9

THE PHONE CALL THAT SAVED OUR MARRIAGE

Cristiane and I never really had what you could call a troubled marriage. On the contrary, we did well most of the time, and those who saw us would have sworn we were the perfect couple. We weren't constantly fighting, there never was any cheating, and we shared the same goals. And yet, from time to time, every four to six months or so, there would be a big falling-out over something. It was as if certain things just sat in the stomach of our relationship for months until they were brought back up and spewed out: things that had never been properly digested or processed between us; roots of problems that we did not know existed and had never cut off.

Sometimes the disagreement was over her jealousy; other times it was because I didn't pay enough attention to her. Now and then the argument was about the work we were doing, or about how I felt disrespected by her, among other things. It was all leaves and branches, and we could not see the roots of the problems.

When we had these big disagreements, we would spend hours speaking our minds in the bedroom. Tempers would flare. She would cry. If she raised her voice, I would raise mine even louder. It would reach a point at which we got tired, or at least I did, and the goal was no longer to solve the problem, but to escape that unpleasant situation. We would skirt the problem, but nothing was ever resolved. I would keep to myself for a few days, and her eyes ended up red from crying, then everything would return to "normal," at least for another four to six months. This was how we spent the first twelve years of our marriage.

In my head, I thought: *She's the problem. I'm not doing anything wrong. She's stubborn and impossible to understand. If I stand my ground, she'll eventually have to give in and change.* And I made no secret of it. On several occasions, I told Cristiane: "You're the one who has the problem! I'm fine. I'm not doing anything wrong. You'd better get your thoughts together and figure this thing out because I don't have time for this." And she would respond with tears or by stating her point of view one more time.

I wasn't trying to be the bad guy. I just really thought that way. It's a hard thing to be sincerely wrong. One awful day, which actually turned into a wonderful day, we had one of those arguments, and the discussion lasted longer than usual. It was late at night, and the end of our argument was nowhere in sight. Then Cristiane had an idea: "I'm going to call my dad." I thought that was a great idea. Right away, I grabbed the phone and handed it to her. "Go ahead, call him! You'll see that I'm right!"

From what I knew of her father, whom I respect very much, and the issue that we were arguing about, I was convinced that he would agree with me and say that she was wrong. Because he had never taken sides before, I saw him as a voice of reason. Though I was embarrassed about taking our problems to him, I saw her decision as a good idea.

I left the room and let her speak to her father. After about five minutes, she came out of the bedroom, calmly handed me the phone and said, "He wants to talk to you."

"Yes, sir," I said.

He went straight for the jugular in a tone that was loud and clear: "Renato, let me tell you something. This is YOUR problem. FIX IT!"

That really took me by surprise. It was not what I was expecting to hear. I thought he would empathize with me. I thought he would say that he'd spoken to her, that now she understood where I was coming from, and I needed to be patient with her. But those words, "this is your problem . . . fix it," were like a red-hot branding iron searing my brain.

He didn't say anything else. I was at a loss for words, and after a few seconds, I said: "I promise you'll never receive another phone call like this because I'll fix it once and for all." I thanked him and hung up the phone.

"This is your problem. Fix it." His words kept ringing in my mind. Suddenly, the scales fell off my eyes. "This is my problem. I have to fix it!" Everything started to become clear to me.

Up to that point, I had always been hammering on the same point, saying to Cristiane: "You're the one who has the problem." The mind-set I had made me view her as the problem, and so I blamed her for failing to solve it. I automatically washed my hands of all blame. *If this marriage fails, it won't be my fault*, I thought.

Besides absolving myself of any responsibility, this mentality made the situation worse in two ways: (1) It gave Cristiane the power to do whatever she wanted about the situation (give up on our marriage, fight for it, continue the way it was), and (2) it gave her the impression that I didn't care about her and wasn't willing to do anything to change the situation.

If she had been another type of woman, she would have taken the power that I had unknowingly placed in her hands, along with the contempt that my attitude conveyed, and would have ended our marriage. Today I understand that if that had happened, I would have been the one to blame. Why? *Because I would not have fulfilled my role as leader and head of my marriage.*

What that phone call taught me was that, as husband, any and every problem that creeps up in my marriage is my problem too.

I cannot assign some problems to me, and others to my wife. Every problem belongs to both of us. If she has a problem, I have a problem. If she's sick, I'm sick. If she has a complaint, I have to find out what it is, and quickly take action at the source of the problem—even if I think it's just her acting like "a woman." This concept changed my perspective on our marriage problems.

As a general rule, I've noticed that men have the tendency to throw a problem back at their wives and continue living their lives as if everything was just fine. A man's nature tends to make him avoid or run away from his wife when she is angry. This is why, whenever a wife confronts her husband with a problem, he automatically points the finger back at his wife and tries to end the conversation. A typical male habit is to take his focus off his wife and place it on his job, sports, TV, video games, etc., as a means of escape. These men need to understand that avoiding or running away from a problem is not going to solve it. Again, I repeat: problems are not like wine.

Men have to take charge of the situation and search for a solution to the problem along with their wife, as any good leader would do. And that's what I did immediately after that phone call.

THE LIST

With her father's blessing, and my new perspective that the problem was mine and it was up to me to solve it, I went back into the room with Cristiane and was logical about things: "Let's make a list of everything that's wrong in our marriage. I want you to tell me everything that you're unhappy about, and I am going to write them down. Then it'll be my turn. When we have the list done, then we'll work together to get rid of each item on it." And we got started. The final score was six to eleven. She had six complaints about me and I had eleven about her. One more and I would have doubled the score. What's most interesting is that when we sat down to make this list, we made more progress in thirty minutes than we had in the first twelve years of our marriage. The effectiveness of reason is so amazing when it comes to problem solving, especially in marriage. That exercise was a pure act of reason, intelligence, and 0% emotion. And that's why we saw positive results. I'm not going to reveal what was on our list, but I can say that it boiled down to two categories:

- Bad attitudes that we were no longer going to have, which saddened or hurt each other.
- Good things that we were going to start doing for each other, things that would please the other person and make them happy.

It was as simple as that. That list helped us to stop looking at each other's flaws and to begin looking at ourselves, at what we had to do to improve our relationship. Now that we had the list, our goals and objectives were clear. We both understood that if we worked together to eliminate each item on the list, each of us doing his or her part without pointing the finger at each other's flaws, we would no longer have those problems. The knowledge that we would no longer have to go through those painful episodes every four to six months was a powerful motivator. I was determined to do everything I had never done to solve our problems once and for all. After all, if the problems went unsolved, the heaviest portion of blame would fall on me because I was the leader and head of my marriage.

And yet, I knew I needed help from above. I couldn't rely solely on my own skills, because the list was long—seventeen items in total, not counting all the little issues related to them . . . It was not going to be easy. We finished our list around 2:30 in the morning and agreed to work on it. I put the list in my pocket, got in the car, and drove to the church where I worked. I wasn't going to wait for the sun to come up; it was now or never.

When I got to the church, all the lights were off, and I headed straight for the altar. No one was there, just God and I. So I poured out my soul to Him. I admitted my mistakes and asked Him for forgiveness, strength, and direction for my life and marriage. I couldn't allow what happened to my parents' marriage happen to mine. I would never accept that, and that's why I was there, asking God to place His hand over Cristiane and me. I held the list up to Him and asked for help. I felt spiritually cleansed. It was a very personal, real moment that I had with God. I left the church feeling relieved and strong.

Though nothing yet had visibly changed, from that moment on everything began to change. I went back home, hugged Cristiane, and we slept in each other's arms. The next day was a new day, the first day of our new marriage. Things didn't change all at once, but we kept applying ourselves to make sure they would. It didn't take very long. Within a few weeks, we noticed that our marriage had been reborn. Up to this very day I still have my list, and as I was writing this chapter, I went back and took a look at it out of curiosity. It was a joy to see, once again, that all the goals we wrote down for each other have been achieved, and many more. Our vicious cycle of problems was broken; the roots were chopped off. That is the power of understanding: "This is YOUR problem. You're the one who has to fix it."

Now that you understand this, I'm going to let Cristiane tell you about the conversation with her father in the next chapter. She's going to tell you how their conversation went during, and after, the phone call—and how it changed her.

TASK:

The list worked for us, and I'm sure it can work for you as well. We often under-estimate the power of writing things down, of putting something on paper. So now I want to encourage you to make your own list. Ask your partner what makes you a difficult person to live with. Write them down regardless of how you feel about them. If your partner agrees to do the same, share your feelings so that he or she can make their own list. Note: this is not an opportunity to attack your partner or to dredge up the past . . . Nor is it the time to get defensive. Your goal in this task is to compile a list of things you will begin working on to solve the problems in your relationship. Periodically, go back and take a look *at this list, dealing with each item until you're finished.*

Decision: From now on, I'm going to work on each item that my spouse and I have agreed to practice or get rid of. These problems are MINE. I will fix them.

/BulletproofMarriage

On our Facebook page
fb.com/BulletproofMarriage
post: *I have written "the list" with my husband/wife. #Bulletproofmarriage*

@BulletproofMate

Tweet: *I have written "the list" with my husband/wife. #BulletproofMarriage @BulletproofMate*

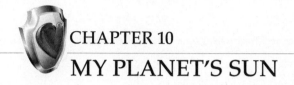

CHAPTER 10
MY PLANET'S SUN

Cristiane says:

When my father answered the phone, I tried to explain what was happening. But I was crying so much that I could hardly even speak. This frequently happens when we talk to relatives about our problems, when emotions cause us to fall apart. He quietly listened and after a few minutes, all he said was: "Give the phone to Renato. Let me talk to him." You already know the rest of the story.

That phone call was the turning point in our marriage, but what really caused me to change was the continuation of that conversation with my father, which we had in person a few days later. The list Renato and I wrote down renewed our commitment to fight for a change and do whatever was necessary to please each other. But inside, I carried a deeper problem; one that I didn't even know existed. I only discovered this problem when my father came to visit and asked me how I had been doing after the phone call.

He never meddled in our marriage, but because of what had happened, it was natural for him to want to know. I replied that I was "trying" to change. I didn't go into details. That was all I said. To be honest, at that moment I was not sure whether or not things had changed. Often in the past, I had told myself that I would change, but several months would pass, and there I would be demanding the same things from Renato all over again. Who could assure me that we would both fulfill our parts to achieve what was on our list?

Sensing uncertainty, my father got straight to the point. I'll never forget that day. We were in the back yard, and he turned to me and said: "Men don't like women who beg for their attention. It makes you undesirable as a woman. Get busy helping others, doing something with your talents, work on your calling."

That was all he said, and that was all I needed to hear. I realized that for all of my marriage, my world had revolved around Renato.

As a pastor's wife I went to church, helped however I could, did the "most" I could; but at the end of the day, my focus was always on Renato. All I wanted was his attention, to be appreciated, to feel like his partner, and to be important to him—which was not too much to ask. But when these things mean everything to you, the issue is elevated to a whole other level. You end up doing everything with that person in mind, and if that person doesn't pay you the attention you expect, everything you've done seems to be for nothing.

Though I was not completely aware of this at the time, it was something I discovered about myself. Instead of taking my place at my husband's side for all those years, I had placed myself behind him. Obviously, he was not going to keep looking back to check up on what I was doing back there. The truth was, I had the wrong idea of what a wife should be for her husband.

I had heard many women say that we should be like the hanger on the back of a picture frame and remain hidden behind them. While our husbands are out front, wives have to remain behind and provide the necessary support for their husbands. This is an old-fashioned idea without any real foundation. I am convinced that many women support the feminist cause for this and other reasons. If I had not woken up to reality, I would have done the same. There comes a time when you get tired of hanging around backstage, feeling less important than your partner, and depending on him for your own sense of self-worth.

Because of my father's words, I finally embarked on an interesting, adventurous, and super-productive journey. I started learning more about myself.

INTRODUCING: CRISTIANE 2.0

I began to develop talents that were hidden or dormant. I invested in helping others and in myself. My self-esteem thanked me every time I took a step toward something new, different, and productive. As I helped others and they found answers, they showed their appreciation, and eventually this helped me overcome all that insecurity I had been carrying inside.

I stopped doing things just to get Renato's attention. I was able to understand him better because we were now in the same boat, working toward the same goals. The only difference was that now I worked as a partner, not behind the scenes. I stopped focusing on him and focused on me, and how I could develop my talents and help others. I came out of my shell. It's amazing how a simple change of focus can transform everything. The problems that previously made me cry and complain became so insignificant that they no longer were worth any of my attention.

One example was the issue of Renato rarely taking me out. Before, I would try to pretend that it didn't matter, but there always came a time when I couldn't pretend any longer, and then suddenly we would have another fight. After my change of focus, this was no longer a problem, nor did I view it as a lack of consideration on his part. I adapted to his tendencies to be a homebody. On our day off, I no longer expected to do anything; I would just find something else to do at home. I made videos on the computer, read books, rented movies, gave myself facials, etc. And guess what happened? I became a much more enjoyable wife.

It wasn't long before Renato noticed this change in me and found me more interesting. What was once rare became a normal part of our daily lives. Conversations were fun, we shared ideas, and talked about our daily experiences, all without me having to force anything. I took my focus off Renato, stopped complaining about everything he was not doing for me, and focused on myself. That is when my eyes were opened, and I was able to see what I was lacking.

For all those years, all Renato needed from me was a partnership. I honestly thought that I was being a partner to him until the point in my life when I discovered that partnership is not chasing after your partner, but walking by his side. This was why he didn't like sharing his day with me and didn't include me in his daily schedule. I wasn't in the same boat with him—I was riding in a dinghy behind his yacht playing catch-up. What I found interesting is that he had previously mentioned me getting more involved in what he was doing . . .

It's one thing to have your partner tell you that you have to change, and quite a different one to finally figure out how you have to change. A simple readjustment of focus transformed our marriage. And when I adapted to Renato's homebody ways, he also adapted to me. We began a healthy competition: who could please each other the most!

I see this problem almost every day in the work I do with women. We seem to have the tendency to focus on others more than we do on ourselves. We can quickly go from one extreme to another. Some women seem to be on hold because of their love life, and others forget about their love life to pursue a career—as if we are unable to do both at the same time and be happy.

This is how many smart women end up becoming frustrated women. No matter how important a career might be, we need a partner to truly enjoy it. And yet, no matter how important our love life might be, we have to have the right perspective about it so we don't become a pain in the neck to the person we love. If you depend on someone else to make you happy, you'll never be able to make anyone happy.

Your world cannot revolve around your partner. He has flaws, he can't always shine his light on your world, and he can't supply everything you need. So it's unwise to put him in that position. You may even be doing everything right, which was what I thought, but you still won't be able to change your situation. Your eyes need to first focus on yourself; only then can there be real and tangible change in your relationship.

I've never forgotten a phrase I heard once in a church meeting: "As long as you keep looking at other people's lives around you, you'll always have problems."

HAVING YOUR OWN LIGHT

I remember speaking to a woman who found out after almost twenty years of marriage that her husband had never loved her. Her world collapsed. Everything kept falling apart until she finally woke up to faith. Many would have made a mess of their lives if they had found themselves in her place. But her story perfectly illustrates what I've just written about.

Imagine a beautiful, intelligent, gifted woman with character to boot—the kind of woman every man is looking for. She spent years of her marriage chasing after her husband, who didn't care about anything she did. Over time, she adapted to his strange ways, never imagining that they might break up in the future. She got married "till death do us part" and endured everything, and then some. Then, one day, out of nowhere, he told her in no uncertain terms that he did not love her.

Instead of realizing what had been going on since the beginning of her marriage, she was surprised, as if he had changed overnight. Why hadn't she noticed this before?

Women whose worlds revolve around their husbands have this disadvantage. They do not properly value themselves, and as a result, they fail to establish boundaries. When you view someone else as more important than you, you cheapen and devalue yourself when you're around them. That person holds all the power in the relationship; if he wants to hurt you, he can do it as many times as he wants because he knows that you'll never, ever, leave. Your life revolves around him, and instead of investing in yourself, in your values and talents, you keep everything locked up inside in a trunk with seven locks on it.

Until she met her husband, that young woman had been full of life, dreams, and plans for the future—an interesting girl who so captivated a boy's heart that he thought, *I want to spend the rest of my life with this woman.* After they were married, she locked everything in a trunk and became a nag. She complained, tried to impose her will in the marriage, and constantly found flaws in everything he did.

She didn't do it on purpose—nobody does. I, for one, did not realize what I was doing. On the contrary, I thought it was my job. It must be a part of our nature as mothers to always seek to make things right, to do something for our children and help them be the best in everything. Except, our husbands are not our children.

I am not saying that this woman's husband stopped loving her because of the way she acted, but it may have contributed a great deal. It's a man's nature to conquer . . . we'll talk more about that in the following chapters. As soon as his wife stops being something that has to be conquered, it's possible he might start looking for other challenges. In other words, she cannot let him feel as if he's the center of her attention.

A woman's value lies in her mystery, her discretion, and the way she blossoms in certain situations. This is exactly what my father advised me to do: men don't like easy women, even when they're their wives. When I began to use my time helping others and developing new talents in the process, Renato began to miss my constant attention. As a result, I became a new conquest for him. I began to shine in my own light.

There is no way for your marriage to blossom over the years when you as a woman do not blossom every day. With every achievement, every book I write, every project I create, I become more confident in myself, and Renato finds me more interesting. I became that young woman Renato met in the beginning: full of dreams, fun, and a great companion for the rest of his life. This is what a partnership should be; this is what it means to be a team.

When Renato first heard that my world used to revolve around him, he glanced at me with a sad look on his face as if he'd just lost a very important position, and asked, "Can I at least be your moon?" Every husband wants your undivided attention, and in the end . . . though our world no longer revolves around them, that doesn't mean we should push them aside and just live our own lives. That's not what I did, and if you do that, you can forget about everything you've learned in this book because your marriage will be doomed.

What we mean is this: if you don't feel good about yourself, if you don't recognize your own self-worth, you will always tend to make your partner your sun—your place of safety, and that is not an intelligent thing to do.

Even if your partner no longer wants to invest in your marriage and has already found another person, don't stop blossoming simply because he's no longer in your life. This woman, whose husband left her after nearly twenty years of marriage, is much more beautiful in every way today, both inside and out. The breakup was actually good for her. The best thing for you to do is to improve while you're still together and possibly even win back your partner's heart.

CLINGY MEN

Women tend to make the man they love into their sun—but hate being the sun themselves. I know . . . I know . . . we love the attention, but when it gets to be too much, it's repulsive. No woman wants a clingy man.

Women want a man who exudes strength, independence, and leadership. We might not always come across this way, especially when we're butting heads with his decisions or complaining that he always does what he wants. But on the other hand, if he starts granting our every wish . . . the relationship starts to deteriorate.

The other day, I was talking to a friend and found something she said about her current relationship very interesting.

"This guy is the 'one,'" Cris. He has what the others didn't have. He's tough."

I was intrigued and wanted to know more. . .

"What do you mean?"

"Well . . . the others always gave in to me, and things just got boring. But this guy's like this . . . I say, 'Let's go this way so we can avoid traffic,' and he says, 'No, I have a route that I like.'"

I realized something I had never noticed before: we, as women, like to test our boundaries and see how far we can go. If a man gives us unlimited freedom, we'll lose all interest! It's not that we like to be controlled . . . but we don't like things to be really easy either. We can get to the point that we stop respecting our beloved partner. And so . . . men, don't feed us grapes while we're lying there with everything at our beck and call. The Cleopatra image is not okay.

The truth is that many men are unable to see their wives' flaws, and as a result, they never help them to improve as people. These men are easily manipulated by them. Every time I made a mistake, I found Renato to be the partner I needed, someone who would point out my mistakes and help me get back in line. Women like that.

 TASK:

In what area and in what way are you sucking the energy out of your partner and becoming problematic for him? Take a few minutes right now to think about this. Write down what you're going to do to behave in a more balanced way in those situations. What talents and healthy activities could you develop so that you're no longer excessively focused on your partner?

_____

_____

_____

I promise to stop making my partner the center of my universe.

/BulletproofMarriage

On our Facebook page
fb.com/BulletproofMarriage
post: *My partner is no longer the center of my universe.*
#Bulletproofmarriage

@BulletproofMate

Tweet: *My partner is no longer the center of my universe.*
#BulletproofMarriage
@BulletproofMate

PART III

TAKING MARRIAGE APART AND PUTTING IT BACK TOGETHER

CHAPTER 11

THE CURSE OF MEN AND WOMEN

Like all other problems of humanity, the love-hate relationship between men and women began in the Garden of Eden. (I hope that Adam and Eve have a special, well-guarded place reserved for them in heaven, because I guarantee you: a lot of people are going to demand explanations from them . . .) Their disobedience opened the way for a curse that directly affected their relationship and those of all their descendants. First, let's understand what happened. I know that you already know the story, but maybe not from this point of view.

Before everything went down the drain in the Garden of Eden, Adam and Eve had a good life in every respect. The Creator had given them a very privileged position of privilege on earth, with the authority to do as they pleased:

. . .let them have dominion over the fish of the sea, over the birds of the air and over the cattle, over all the earth and over every creeping thing that creeps on the earth. So God created man in His own image; in the image of God He created him; male and female He created them. Then God blessed them, and God said to them, "Be fruitful and multiply; fill the earth and subdue it; have dominion over the fish of the sea, over the birds of the air, and over every living thing that moves on the

earth." And God said, "See, I have given you every herb that yields seed which is on the face of all the earth, and every tree whose fruit yields seed; to you it shall be for food. Also, to every beast of the earth, to every bird of the air, and to everything that creeps on the earth, in which there is life, I have given every green herb for food"; and it was so. (Genesis 1:26–30)

Man was given dominion over every animal and plant and over all the earth. This authority was shared with his wife: *". . .and God said to them . . ."* This means that all of nature was meant to serve men and women. Nature was meant to serve them and meet all their needs.

And so, this beautiful couple literally lived in paradise and enjoyed power, harmony, and the presence of God. They had no bills to pay, and they did not point fingers at each other's flaws. Adam had the woman he had asked God for, and Eve had the man who . . . well, the only one around. In any case, they were a couple with no problems.

But something had to go wrong, and to make matters worse, that day a snake came into the garden. Eve disobeyed God and led her husband to do the same. Time to settle the score.

First, God called out to Adam, who was quick to blame Eve. However, the Lord did not buy that idea, thus stressing the point that a leader is responsible for everything that happens under his responsibility. Remember chapter 9, "This Is YOUR problem?" Adam had to learn this the hard way. As a result of his failure and disobedience, God declared:

Because you have heeded the voice of your wife, and have eaten from the tree of which I commanded you, saying, "You shall not eat of it": Cursed is the ground for your sake, in toil you shall eat of it all the days of your life. Both thorns and thistles it shall bring forth for you, and you shall eat the herb of the field. In the sweat of your face you shall eat bread till you return to the ground, for out of it you were taken; for dust you are and to dust you shall return. (Genesis 3.17–19)

In turn, Eve blamed the serpent. But it was not a good day for excuses:

To the woman He said: I will greatly multiply your sorrow and your conception; in pain you shall bring forth children; your desire shall be for your husband and he shall rule over you. (v. 16)

It's interesting to note that as a result of the curse, man and woman now became subject to the elements from which they came—the elements from which they were created: man was subjected to the dust of the ground, and woman was subjected to man, and this is where the man-woman curse[5] began. Let's understand the impact and consequences of this curse in a marriage.

A SLAVE TO HIS WORK

The curse that struck man was directly related to his work. Before the curse, there was harmony and full cooperation between man and the earth; but after the curse, the ground became man's enemy. Cooperation was no more. Instead, there would now be difficult, hard labor—a struggle between nature and man. It was as if the earth would now reluctantly give its fruit to man, and frequently produce thorns instead of fruit.

This hardship would last a lifetime, until he would finally lose the battle and return to where he had come from: the dust of the ground.

---

[5] Let me clarify: a careful analysis of the biblical text will reveal that God did not curse Adam and Eve. The text says that God cursed the serpent and the ground, not the human being. But even though man and woman were not directly cursed, they clearly suffered the consequences of these two curses, to which I refer henceforth in the singular: "The curse of men and women."

(Note that up to this point there was no death. Man had been created to live forever, but sin limited his time on earth. When God joined Adam and Eve together in the beginning, the plan had not been "till death do us part" but rather "for all eternity".)

Consider one of the aggravating factors: man had been appointed provider of his family. This meant there was no way to escape the curse. He had to work—and he had to get his sustenance now from the ground that had become his enemy. The pressure of supporting his family, being the hunter, supplying his family with everything they need, drives man to demand fruit for his labor. It's a matter of honor, pride, the respect of your wife's parents, and his own self-worth. The instinct of wanting to prove himself through his work and achievements is in the very DNA of every man.

This is why the greatest frustration a man has to endure is professional failure. He may lose his marriage, be separated from his children, and laid up with a disability, but he can endure all this as long as he feels useful and is a success at work. This doesn't mean he'll be happy, but his achievements at work will feed his ego more than anything else. This is his curse, his burden.

This curse makes him always feel dissatisfied no matter how much he has achieved. You hardly will ever hear men say, "I've done all I ever dreamed of doing. I'm going to quit now." If he works day and night to reach a goal, applies all his energy and gets good results, he will typically say, "It could have been better." He never feels that he's made it. He's always demanding more of himself.

It's a common fact that many men develop depression when they retire, some get sick and even die shortly afterward. It's as if their jobs were their life. Many refuse to retire and continue working for as long as their health allows.

Besides this dissatisfaction, men also compare themselves to more successful men and want to surpass them—or feel less of a man if they can't be as good as them. Men's competitive spirit is unlike anything else. No wonder the Guinness Book of World Records is filled mostly with men, especially when it comes to competitive activities. For you to have a better idea of what I'm talking about, there's a category in the book where men broke sixteen different records, one by a team of twelve German gymnasts . . . What was the challenge? "The most somersaults in underpants in ninety seconds." This team has remained unbeaten since 2011, with ninety-five. This is the type of thing you would not find twelve women willing to compete for.

So how does this affect a relationship?

You may have already guessed it. Isn't the amount of time a man spends at his work one of the classic complaints of wives? Isn't the "tendency to spend" (the money he earns by the sweat of his brow) one of the main complaints that men have about their wives? Now you know why.

In the beginning of a relationship, while they're dating, men see women as a conquest, a job to be completed. It's a competition—who will win the girl? Who will she choose as her boyfriend? This motivates him to work for her attention and heart. But when he finally conquers her and they get married, he turns his attention to the next challenge, which almost always has to do with his job. This is why he plunges into work and leaves his wife at home dying from a lack of attention. When she complains, he gives her a puzzled look and asks, "Don't you understand that I have to work, and that I'm doing all this for you?" He gets it right with the first part of his answer, but not exactly with the second part. He works for his own sake more than he does for hers.

The curse of work makes men slaves to a sense of accomplishment, which they rarely achieve. During his search for this sense, he sacrifices family, wife, health, and anything else. Ask a husband to talk to his wife about the family and their relationship, and he'll be unable to come up with anything to talk about. Ask him to talk to his friends about work, and he won't be able to stop.

A wife can easily misinterpret this behavior and assume her husband does not love her because he doesn't spend time with or talk to her; and because he seems happier at work and with his friends than with her and things that are related to her. But it would be a mistake for her to take this personally and assume that something is wrong with him, or with her. What should she do? How can she deal with this curse and help her husband at the same time? First of all, it's important for her to understand the curse that fell upon her.

HER HUSBAND'S ATTENTION

The curse that fell upon the woman is related to her need for her husband's attention and approval. Putting aside the part about the pains of childbirth, which this book does not intend to solve (sorry, women!), the second part of the curse says: *your desire shall be for your husband, and he shall rule over you.* This means you are always going to want something from your husband, and he will be your leader. Just as man became a slave to his work, subject to the dust of the ground, she became dependent on her husband's approval, dependent on him for the fulfilment of her desires and dreams.

Up to that moment, man and woman had never worried about "who's in charge." It was a harmonious union without the resistance of one or the impositions of the other. The two were one. But now, because of the woman's mistake, she was intentionally placed under the care and leadership of her husband, as if to remind her of the mistake she made by persuading him to sin.

I know this concept is taboo for most women, but the truth is, it could have been much worse. Just think: she's placed under the man who *loves her*? It would have been much worse if she had been placed under someone who *hated her* . . . Be that as it may, the concept of submission is a subject for a later chapter, which we hope will clarify the issue for you and remove the venom that's been injected into the word by feminist ideologies.

What this curse caused in women was the need to have their husband's absolute total attention. She wants to be his princess, the chosen one, the most desired woman in the world, the one he risks his life for, and his reason for leaving everything and everyone he likes just to be at her side. And yet, she is rarely able to hold that kind of attention for very long. Under the effects of his own curse, he is concentrating on his work, his next conquest, and still resents her when she demands his attention. He sees her as interfering with his goals. He gets upset because she doesn't "understand" that he has to work, and feels she doesn't properly appreciate him for all his hard work and dedication.

In her serach for her husband's attention, a woman unknowingly puts her self-worth on hold and does everything she can to attract his attention. She spends money on attractive, seductive clothing, physical beauty, makeup, hair . . . but this is only just the beginning. She cries, becomes a drama queen, makes herself out to be a victim, gets jealous, is demanding, tries to emotionally blackmail her husband, stops taking care of her home, competes with her mother-in-law and even with the dog. . . These days, many unhappily married women are even capable of having an affair simply to get their husband's attention.

This desperate yearning causes many women, considered intelligent and talented in their fields, to put up with men who treat them badly, in exchange for a little attention. This was the case of Rosanne, whom we recently helped in our counseling office.

She's an accountant. At the age of thirty-four, she is the pride of her family because she's achieved so much in her career. She opened her own practice two years ago. She has more than fifty clients and employs a staff of five. She's a determined and capable woman. But while she abounds in determination and confidence for business, she lacks them in her love life.

Rosanne has been in an on-again-off-again relationship with Roger. He is thirty-one years old, has no achievements to speak of, and is the embodiment of the perfect Casanova. He's handsome, tall, and charming—a smooth talker who knows exactly what women want to hear.

Roger has no steady job or profession—unless slacker can be considered a profession. If it were up to him, there would even be a union for slackers by now. He's a talented storyteller who stars as both hero and victim in his stories. His mother pays his rent while he waits for the "perfect" job to come along. His dad pays for his car because "he can't get around if he doesn't have a car."

Rosanne gives him love, good food when he comes to visit, sex, and even buys clothes for him. Her boyfriend has to dress well.

In return, Roger has already cheated on her at least three times, that she knows of. He tells her he's not "ready" for marriage. Every now and then he shows up at Rosanne's office, tells her one of his stories, and convinces her to write him a check, between a few hugs and kisses, swearing that this money is all he needs to start an exciting new business venture.

Rosanne is like many other intelligent and talented women who fail to see how foolish they are when it comes to love.

Why do they subject themselves to this? It's the curse of women.

TWO FOR THE PRICE OF ONE

The two curses affecting men and women are, in fact, one curse: insecurity.

At the core, men are unsure of themselves. Clearly, some show it more than others, but all men suffer from the same problem, even men who appear to be tough and extremely brave, or those with strong personalities. This behavior can actually be a mask to hide their insecurity. Whether or not they are conscious of it, man shoulders the burden of the rejection he suffered in Eden, where he was the main offender.

A fear of failure, poverty, and inadequacy drives him to work himself to death. The voice of a demanding parent as a child still echoes in his ear and makes him feel as if he will never measure up to his or her expectations, no matter how successful he might be.

The pride that holds him back from acknowledging his mistakes and learning from others gets stronger when he sees other men succeeding where he has failed. Anger, aggression, addictions, lies, and other self-destructive behaviors are simply his way of dealing with the deep insecurities he feels deep insde. They are simply his attempts at covering the nakedness of his insecurity with fig leaves.

A woman's insecurity is easier to identify than a man's because she finds it easier to express her emotions. I know beautiful women who think they're ugly because one part of their body does not conform to the standards that women's magazines set. Others are jealous of anything their husband pays attention to. They are jealous of his job, football team, sister-in-law, car, the woman standing at the bus stop, colleague at work, ex-girlfriend—anything their husbands pay the least bit of attention to, and even what he doesn't—because of their insecurity.

Most women have low self-esteem. The same way many men use masculinity, strength, and a strong temperament to mask their insecurity, many women rebel against their curse and declare themselves independent of men. "I don't need a man to be happy," "All men are the same—they can't be trusted." "No man will ever boss me around, and similar phrases form their mind-set. However, deep down they remain unhappy.

In summary: they are both desperately insecure and in need of reassurances from each other. (Two thumbs up to Adam and Eve. Thanks a million!)

Now the most important question: how do you get rid of this curse?

CHAPTER 12

FREEDOM FROM THE CURSE

I have good news and bad news. Let's start with the bad news. The first thing that men and women have to understand is that they are not going to change each other. Men will always be driven by their achievements at work, and women will always be driven by a desire to be the focus of man's attention. It's useless to fight against these facts. Those who resist move to the other extreme, which is no better. Men stop conquering and become weak, fragile, and a disgrace to themselves and their family; women become bitter, hard, unapproachable by men, and lonely. It's futile to rebel against the curse. You have to learn to deal with it—yours and your spouse's.

Now the good news: there are effective ways to deal with the curse. There are two aspects—one aspect, only you can deal with; the other, only God can do.

Let's take a look at what a husband can do and how his wife can help him.

THE STRATEGY FOR MEN

Throughout the Bible, God teaches men the key to being successful, which can be summarized in these words: "Work in partnership with Me." One of the clearest passages about this is found in Psalm 127:1–2:

*Unless the L*ORD *builds the house, they labor in vain who build it; unless the L*ORD *guards the city, the watchman stays awake in vain. It is vain for you to rise up early, to sit up late, to eat the bread of sorrows; for so He gives His beloved sleep.*

There is the secret! God clearly says that men have to work in partnership with Him. Their success depends on their relationship with the Creator. Though they have to work, they cannot simply rely on their own skills. They have to also depend on God. When men work in partnership with Him, they don't have to worry about the result. After all, their Partner works even while they sleep! For this reason, there is no excessive self-criticism, insecurity, or depression because of what appear to be disappointing results. Men are no longer slaves to their work because they understand that their Partner is more concerned about their growth. They have confidence, peace, and the assurance that the future will be bright.

Women can help men by reminding them of the importance of this dependence. In addition to praying for success in their jobs, they should wisely encourage their husbands to have a relationship with God, because they will also benefit from this. The message that women must convey to them, in their own words, is: "By yourself, you can only achieve what is possible. With God, you achieve the impossible."

Another concept that men have to take in and practice to counteract the effects of their curse is balance. Men need to remember that there will always be work to do, and no matter how much we work, our work will never be done. If we work for twenty-for hours straight, the next day there will still be more work to be done. Men, especially married men, have to keep in mind that they have other more important things in their lives, such as their wives. And so, they need to be balanced.

The Bible says that God created the Sabbath for "man."[6] I believe He referred specifically to men, even more than women, because He knew that if He did not specify the Sabbath as a day of rest that men would work seven days a week. God did not need to order men to work; instead, He had to command them to rest.

Women understand the idea of the Sabbath only too well. If Cristiane would not remind me and plan something relaxing for us to do for at least a couple of hours a week, I would only stop working to eat and sleep. In the beginning of our marriage, I resisted her attempts. I was unbalanced, working practically seven days a week. I would tell her that she had to get used to it, fit into my routine and conform. She wanted a little of my attention, but I would give her practically none, and then I would get upset when she insisted that I spend time with her.

Men need to accept this help from women. They are a God-given resource to help them with their problem of balance. If your wife is complaining that you do not spend enough time with her or your children, that you are working too hard, etc., she is probably right. Listen to her. Be balanced.

Another issue that every man needs to be very careful about in order to not worsen the curse is comparing themselves to others. Some competition is good. Having a mentor or role models who motivate you are positive things, but be careful not to constantly compare yourself to others! Comparing yourself to other men and measuring your success with theirs is the best recipe for frustration and insecurity.

We have to trust and develop the talents we possess, and not attempt to copy others. Learn more about yourself, develop your own identity, pinpoint your talents, and work on them. Learn to celebrate the success of others, as well as your own. Learn to congratulate yourself for your accomplishments. Isn't that what God did when He created

---

[6] Mark 2:27.

the world? The account of the Creation states that at the end of each day, God looked at His works and saw that *"it was good."*[7] (And though He is God, He set aside one day at the end of that week to rest.) When men put this into practice, it acts as a strong antidote for the curse.

This is one of the most important roles wives can have to help their husbands. First, they should never, ever, compare them to other men. They should never say, "You should be more like my father . . ." or "So-and-so's husband is really nice . . ." Ladies, this will never get you the result you're looking for. Do you really think those comments will motivate them to be better men? The truth is, they are like a dagger to their pride and self-esteem. This is worth repeating because it's so important: never compare your husband (or son) to another man, not even in your dreams.[8]

Instead of comparing him to someone else, recognize and praise his qualities and achievements. Don't criticize and point out his failures in a negative manner. Be an encouraging voice by having confidence in his abilities. This is essential in good times, and especially important in bad times. Nothing brings a man down more than professional failure. Do you want to see a depressed man? Fire him from his job. But you don't have to go that far; just point out a mistake he made at work. After work, he'll go straight to the bar or plop down in front of the TV and feel like he's the worst creature in the world. Many men don't even tell their wives that they've been fired. They leave in the morning as if they were going to work as usual, when in fact they're searching for

---

[7] Genesis 1:18.

[8] A civil war erupted and dragged on for years in Israel when women negatively compared King Saul to David. Right after David defeated Goliath and the Philistine army, he returned to Jerusalem victorious with King Saul and his army. Welcoming them with a great celebration, the women sang: "Saul killed thousands, but David killed tens of thousands!" (1 Samuel 18:7). King Saul, insecure as he was, couldn't take that unfavorable comparison, and his reaction to it hastened his tragic demise.

another job. In a situation like this, a woman can either raise her husband up or finish him off and bury him.

This reminds me of Cristina, the wife of the great Brazilian basketball player of international fame, Oscar Schmidt. During her interview for The Love School, she told us that three months shy of getting a degree in psychology, she chose to drop out (after five years of college) and move to Italy with her husband where he had been hired to play. Cristina said that one motivation was the thought of her husband facing all the struggles and challenges of a new country while she was far away finishing college in Brazil. And so, she decided to prioritize her marriage. She left everything behind, went to Italy with him, and never finished her degree. As she had anticipated, Oscar's team lost the first seven games he played. But with his wife by his side, he got back up and had a brilliant thirteen-year career in Italy, not to mention the international titles he won for Brazil. He was the highest scoring basketball player, an absolute success not only on the courts but also at home. He credits his wife for this: "Without her support, I would never have accomplished what I did," he said. The couple has been together for over thirty-seven years.

Cristiane:

It's common for women to think that praising our spouses will cause their egos to go through the roof. Women are afraid that their husbands will become arrogant and self-sufficient. But this fear is a reflection of our own insecurity. We think that one compliment will make them think they're better than us. This is why many women admire their husbands, but almost never verbalize their admiration.

But with this new understanding that men are always chasing after achievement, recognition, and self-approval, you can see how important it is for you to be at his side.

One thing I always saw in my mother was her appreciation and admiration for my father. She didn't pretend to be blind to his mistakes, but her praise was so much more frequent that my father's flaws seemed irrelevant and insignificant. This made my sister and me respect and admire him too, and was an example of how we should treat our future husbands. This is something Renato never had to deal with.

When a woman becomes her husband's number-one fan, she also wins, and in a big way. It's like a football game. When he scores and wins the game, he'll immediately run to her outstretched arms and celebrate. When he loses, he'll also run into her arms knowing that she will not be critical of him. She'll give him an encouraging word, and the loving look in her eyes will melt away all his sadness. Now, who doesn't want that from their favorite player? Our female nature loves this masculine "dependency"!

This is where many women make the mistake, not because they want to, but because they think they need to be tough with their husbands. You tell him how handsome he is, and he rolls his eyes as if the compliment is ridiculous. If you fall for that "tough" male exterior, you might convince yourself that he doesn't need your compliments. But you would be wrong. He needs them in a big way. Men pretend to be tough, but deep down they want your compliments. Besides, who else will say these things to him except you and his mother? His co-workers?

When they don't react the way we would react, that doesn't mean they don't like it. Anyone can criticize him, but your criticism will be far more painful. The words of a man's wife will always hold more weight. Don't forget that.

When a woman supports her husband in victory and defeat, he'll never abandon her, unless he's a fool (in this case, he'll be doing her a favor).

THE STRATEGY FOR WOMEN

A woman's curse makes her dependent on a husband for her own sense of happiness and accomplishment. She will look for him for total fulfilment. But let's make one thing clear here: *no man can satisfy all the needs and expectations of a woman*. No man in the world could do this, not even if he were designed and created by a woman (her creation would be another woman, which she would also find unsatisfying).

The truth is, no man can satisfy all the needs of a woman, nor can a woman satisfy all the needs of a man. That would be utopia. Here's what I hear a lot: "I'm looking for someone who will complete me," or "My husband doesn't complete me." Stop right there. This person who "completes" you does not exist. Our life is made complete through a combination of things, not by one person. And no matter how complete a person's life may be, they will always have problems.

Women: Don't demand something from your husband that he's unable to give. Your husband is not responsible for making you happy, and you are not responsible for making him happy. Singles reading this book in preparation for marriage: if you consider yourself an unhappy person, please don't get married! Spare that other person from a life of misery. First you have to resolve your own problems, become a happy person, and then get married and share your happiness with someone else. Happiness in marriage is produced by a number of things, one of which is your husband. But there are things that he cannot do for you. For example, I cannot give my wife the things that God gives her. I'm not God. He gives Cristiane things I can't even imagine she needs, when she needs them, such as comfort, wisdom, and peace. I cannot give her motherly advice. This is something she can only get from her mother. I cannot make her feel more useful and valued than what I already do. But when she receives feedback from others she has helped through her work, her sense of self-worth increases. All these things begin to add up and help to make her a happy person—so that she no longer depends solely on me to make her happy.

A woman needs to understand that hoping to have all her needs fulfilled by a man is a curse in itself. Therefore, she needs to learn not to set herself up for the curse. Women need to discover those things that bring them fulfilment, like having a personal relationship with God, their job, a proper sense of self-worth. This will help you to stop smothering your husband, and he will start to find you more interesting and attractive.

Stop the excessive focus on your husband. Don't be like an octopus, clinging to him with all your tentacles. Don't suffocate him (one of the most common complaints I hear from husbands).

No value is placed on things that come easy. No one fights for what is easy. When a woman is too easy, she becomes boring and will get the opposite of what she's looking for: a man's disdain. But when she holds back and gives herself to him bit by bit, it keeps him interested in the chase. For example, don't insist that he take you out on a date. Drop hints of what you like and want, but don't beg for attention. A wise woman will make a man work to get her. A relationship has to involve motivation and the feeling of achievement for a man, just like his job. At times it's good for him to come looking for you.

Freedom from the curse means returning to the original state, before the fall in Eden: man should go back to having dominion over the earth, instead of being its slave, and woman should go back to her position as man's helper and teammate.

When she becomes his helper in reaching his goals, she becomes extremely valuable to him, and this is when she'll get what she wants the most: his attention. Some wives prefer to compete with their husbands rather than join their teams. They make the main focus of their lives revolves around something that does not help their husbands in anything. When a woman refuses to help and, on top of it all, gives her husband a hard time, she is shooting herself in the foot: she will become unattractive to him.

Cristiane:

Our problem is that we don't believe in ourselves. We always put ourselves down with words and thoughts. Many women think this is being humble, but it has nothing to do with it. This "humility" is annoying and detrimental for a relationship.

If you do not learn to appreciate yourself as a woman, all outward efforts are useless. You will be unable to appreciate anything else in life and will become a difficult person to live with. I've been there. I had everything, the wedding of my dreams, an exemplary family, health, and even natural beauty, but I did not value myself. So I would try to manipulate things. I would constantly point out problems in my marriage because Renato was not giving me the attention I wanted. I would accuse him of not loving me, and one day I reached the last straw that I even asked him if he wanted a divorce.

I could not see my own beauty. I would constantly change my looks, try different styles, and never thought I was pretty. I have photos from that time, and when I look at the clothes I'm wearing in the pictures, I ask myself what must have been going on in my mind to wear those clothes. It's amazing how frivolous things like clothing and hairstyle can reveal insecurities. When I remember those times, I do not understand why I was so blind.

Only after I learned to truly appreciate myself, as I explained in chapter 10, did I change. It was as if my eyes had been closed until then. I was able to see my potential—and what potential! If women knew their potential, they would not degrade themselves as much as they do nowadays . . .

"Who can find a virtuous wife? For her worth is far above rubies."
Proverbs 31.10

You can be this virtuous woman, which I like to call a "V Woman." All you need to do is believe and demonstrate your worth by what you do and who you are.

How can a husband help his wife get rid of her curse?

He has to reassure her in every possible way. For example: don't pay attention to other women, pay her compliments about her character and beauty, put her before everything and everyone, seek out and value her opinion, help her to invest in her talents and potential. In other words, pump up your wife's self-worth. Men cannot expect their wives to get rid of the curse on their own without their help. Leaving your wife alone with her problems and struggles is not a wise thing to do. Sometimes, women seek out help from others because their husbands are not there for them (he may resent her for this, but it was really due to his negligence). Support and genuine recognition from her husband is much more valuable to her than anyone else's support. But if she sees him being extremely helpful to others, but not to her, her insecurities will only increase.

Husbands need to understand that they are gaining by investing in their wives. There is an interesting verse in Proverbs that says:

Where no oxen are, the trough is clean, but much increase comes by the strength of an ox.[9]

---

[9] Proverbs 14:4.

Meaning: if you have no oxen, you won't have ox poo to clean up, but neither will you enjoy a harvest. If you want an abundant harvest, you have to be ready to clean up after the oxen . . . This is an insight into marriage. It takes work, at times it stinks, you have to clean up messes, but the end result is truly good. A happy marriage takes work. Men: this should be good news for us . . . We love to work, don't we?

COMPENSATING

Now that you understand the curse that plagues men and women, you can better understand why you and your spouse do the things you do. And now that you understand what you're each dealing with, you should help each other make the proper adjustments.

Mature and successful marriages come from those those who learn to create this balance and work at helping each other.

TASK:

Meditate on what you have read in this chapter and the previous one. How have the effects of these curses affected you and your spouse? Write down what they are and how you will deal with them from now on . . . instead of continuing what you have been doing.

/BulletproofMarriage

On our Facebook page
fb.com/BulletproofMarriage
post: *Now I know how to deal with the curse.*
#Bulletproofmarriage

@BulletproofMate

Tweet: *Now I know how to deal with the curse.*
#BulletproofMarriage
@BulletproofMate

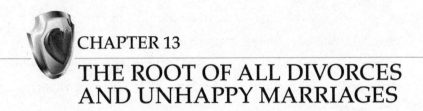

CHAPTER 13

THE ROOT OF ALL DIVORCES AND UNHAPPY MARRIAGES

If you were to ask a group of divorced people what led to the collapse of their marriages, you would get a number of different responses. Many would blame their spouse's infidelity, others would say they were incompatible; others would cite financial issues, yet others would blame their partner's lack of commitment. If we were to ask unhappy couples to list the reasons for their unhappiness, they would say things like "He doesn't pay attention to me," "I don't trust him anymore," "We fight all the time," "She's stubborn." and so on. Obviously, the reasons for an unhappy marriage are not always the same, nor are the reasons for divorce. But they all have one main root. The reasons couples give are simply consequences of a deeper problem, which is the root of all unhappy marriages and divorces. Psychologists and marriage therapists will not reveal this root to you. But the Author of marriage has already revealed it.

Identifying this root and cutting it out of your life is so effective that even if this is the only thing you learn from this book, you will have the power to transform your marriage.

POWERLESS TO STOP DIVORCE

In order to identify this deep root, I would like to point you to two passages from the Bible that may seem inconsistent at first glance. In the first, God allows divorce in the Law of Moses, in the first few books of the Old Testament. Second, in the last book of the Old Testament[10] we discover that God hates divorce.[11] Yes, that's the word He uses: *hate*. It is rare to see in the Bible that God hates something. When He uses this word, He means it. He really *hates* divorce. Why is that?

When a couple gets divorced, they might as well look God in the face, and say, "Look, Lord, You made a mistake. This marriage thing doesn't work." Divorce is an insult to God, since it was He who initiated the covenant of marriage. It's a sharp deviation from what He originally had in mind when He joined man and woman.

But if this is God's view of divorce, why did He make an exception for it in the law He created? If He's the Almighty and truly hates divorce, why doesn't He stop it?

This was the question that religious leaders asked Jesus. Unlike you, they were not interested in knowing the answer. They simply wanted to trick Him into saying something that could be used against Him in court—literally. As always, they got more than they bargained for and Jesus' answer provided us a wonderful revelation about a controversial subject:

> One day the Pharisees were badgering him: "Is it legal for a man to divorce his wife for any reason?" He answered, "Haven't you read in your Bible that the Creator originally made man and woman for each other, male and female? And because of this, a man leaves father and mother and is firmly bonded to his wife, becoming one flesh—no longer two bodies but one. Because God created this organic union of the two sexes, no one should desecrate his art by cutting them apart." Matthew 19.3–6 (MSG)

---

[10] Deuteronomy 24:1.
[11] Malachi 2:16.

With this reply, Jesus points out God's original plan and reveals the true meaning of marriage. In the mathematics of God: $1 + 1 = 1$. In other words, when a man and woman are united in marriage, they become one person. The fusion of two individuals creates a whole new person. I am no longer the person I was when I was single, nor is Cristiane. Those who knew us when we were single can clearly see this today. We became different people (much better people) because of our marriage. There was a fusion of personalities. We often use the analogy of mashed potatoes, which nicely demonstrates this process. Two potatoes are just that: two potatoes. But when you mash them and add milk and butter, they become another element altogether: mashed potatoes. Mashed potatoes are no longer milk, butter, or just potatoes . . . There is no way to separate these three elements. That is exactly what Jesus meant by *"no longer two bodies but one."*

The Hebrew word for "bonded" in the original text comes from the word for "glue," in the sense that two objects are joined together in a way that they can no longer be separated without causing damage to each other. Imagine tearing apart your own flesh. That's what happens in a divorce. It causes deep wounds that are difficult to heal, and great suffering in the lives of those involved. Marriage was designed to create a fusion, resulting in a third element—never to be torn apart.

Many want to get married, but remain the same person they were when they were single. They resist the merging process and never become one flesh. They remain two distinct, unchangeable individuals within the relationship. This relationship is never going to work. I'm not suggesting that you give up your own personality and stop being you. The idea is to improve who you are by allowing your partner to influence you, by molding yourself around him or her. It's like a child. He has characteristics of both parents—his dad's nose, mother's eyes, dad's hair, and mother's skin tone, etc.—but he also has his own personality. The same goes for marriage. You end up a product of your union. And so, when you get married, you have to have a "we" rather than a "me" mindset.

When you try to justify your mistakes to your partner and say: "This is the way I am. I was born like this, I grew up like this, I've always been like this, and I'm always going to be like this . . . This is who I am"—you maintain a death grip on your individuality at the expense of your marriage. If the way you are is not good for your relationship, you have to find a way to change it—or there will be no way for your marriage except the highway!

"This is how I am," was my favorite sentence to end an argument with Cristiane. I would ask, "Why are you trying to change me? You knew I was like this when you met me." That was the voice of my individuality resisting the bonding into one flesh. Many listen to this voice until finally they reach a point and divorce. Why all the stubbornness? It is because of the root that Jesus reveals below.

A HEART OF STONE

Continuing from the previous passage:

They shot back in rebuttal, "If that's so, why did Moses give instructions for divorce papers and divorce procedures?" Jesus said, "Moses provided for divorce as a concession to your hardheartedness, but it is not part of God's original plan. I'm holding you to the original plan. Matthew 19.7–9 (MSG)

Here is the real root of every divorce and unhappy marriage: hardness of heart. Divorce was not a part of God's original plan. It was not an option when He created marriage. However, because of man's rock-hard heart, He had to tolerate—even allow—something He hates. Think about that for a minute. When you harden your heart, not even God can prevent divorce from happening to you! But aren't all things possible for

Him? Why doesn't He prevent this thing that He hates? And worse yet, He made it legal! Couldn't He have forbidden it from the beginning? God is not a tyrant. He respects our choices. He would never force His way into our hearts and make us change. But if God cannot help when you are hard-hearted, what about your spouse? You're the only one who can do something about this and avoid the disaster.

But first you need to understand what hard-heartedness is. What causes hardness of heart? Could you be hard-hearted and not know it?

A great many things can cause hardness of heart. When we speak about the heart, we're referring to the center of emotions and feelings inside of us. Any negative feeling that has not been properly processed and eliminated ends up turning our hearts into stone. One in particular is pride.

Pride turns hearts into concrete. Proud people are blind to their mistakes. In general, they think they are unusually humble and that everyone else is at fault. They are always the misunderstood victims; they don't like to admit their mistakes and would rather have a tooth pulled without anaesthesia than to apologize. Because they are always right, proud people wait for others to give in and back off. They can't see how important it is for someone who's been hurt to have their offender acknowledge their mistake and apologize. Many problems would be quickly solved if the proud person would simply say: "I'm sorry. I messed up. I won't do that again." Instead, the proud choose to further harden their hearts.

I remember an elderly couple whose marriage had been arranged when the girl was fourteen. The family was worried about her strong personality and thought that marriage would be a good way to "domesticate" her. Poor guy! They had their first fight on their honeymoon (did you expect it would take longer than that?). He said something silly about his childhood sweetheart being the only girl he had ever loved, and how he used to bring her fruits as gifts when he was ten years old. This "revelation" hurt her and stayed bottled up inside for decades: "He doesn't love me. He'll never love me." He never apologized because he felt she was being silly. She did everything in her power to make his life a living hell because she had felt hurt.

What did they gain by doing this? A ruined marriage . . . a shattered family . . . years of unnecessary suffering. He looked elsewhere for the attention he wasn't getting at home, and she put up with her husband's many affairs, piling one hurtful feeling on top of another toward "the other woman." Though they loved each other, neither one of them gave in. Life passed them by and only toward the very end did they realize that they'd missed out on being happy all those years they had been together.

Proud people miss out on so many opportunities! Little do they know that if they weren't so hard, they would be much happier. They could learn new things, discover new ways of looking at life . . . Why do you think God decided to have two so very different beings, such as man and woman, live together?

If you think about it, it might seem like marriage is God's way of playing a cruel joke on us. It's almost as if the Father, Son, and Holy Spirit got to laughing one day, rubbed their hands together, and said: "Here's an idea! Let's create man. He could be like this and that . . . Okay! Now let's create woman . . . she could be . . . the exact opposite! Let's see what happens! They'll have to live in the same house. Oh, and let's make a rule: they can't ever separate!" It seems like a joke! But it's very clear, fortunately, that there is an actual purpose for marriage.

God allows two completely different people to live together, not to torture the people He created, but rather that each one would challenge the other to become a better person. He made us different so that we would complement each other. But you can only live with your spouse and improve as a person when your heart is open and flexible.

You need a good dose of humility to kill this bad root and enjoy the best of what marriage has to offer.

Let us take another look at the elderly couple's example. The problem started when the husband made a dumb comment. If he had swallowed his pride and made a heartfelt apology to his wife, he would have avoided fifty years of living hell. On the other hand, if she had refused to take his dumb comment so seriously and treated her husband with respect and affection, he would have had no choice but to make her happy.

Selfishness, pride's cousin, also has the power to harden a heart. A selfish person is guided by the following sayings: *what matters is what I want, what is good for me, and my wishes first*. A selfish person doesn't care about another person's point of view. He hears but doesn't listen, because his ego speaks louder than anyone else and drowns out his partner's voice.

In the beginning of my marriage, I wasn't concerned about the needs of my wife. As long as I was happy at work, everything was just fine. I thought that as long as she had everything she needed at home, she had no reason to complain. If you believe your spouse has nothing to complain about because you buy her this or give her that . . . then understand this: what's the point in giving your spouse a lot of what she already has, and none of what she really needs and feels she's lacking?

I met a young man who thought his wife was extremely happy. Then one day he got a shock when his wife announced that she was leaving him. Conspiracy theories began to pop up in his mind. Who had talked his perfect and submissive wife into leaving him after six years? Was it her brother? One of her friends? The pastor? The son from her first marriage whom he'd never got along with? It was so unfair, he thought. He had been such a great husband, always given her everything, stood by her side, was consistently nice to her, and now she was going to leave him without a single explanation as to why.

What he did not realize was that she had felt left out for most of their years of marriage. She admitted to me that everything her husband did and said revolved around him. He never was interested in what she liked or wanted. They did not communicate, and he felt he was much smarter than her—at least that's the impression he gave—and he would force her to accompany him on cultural tours, something she had no interest in whatsoever. She was wrong for never letting him know that she didn't like any of the things they did together. But if he had looked past his own nose, he would have noticed that there was an unhappy, neglected woman at his side.

Make a note of this: you gave up the right to think only about yourself the day you signed your marriage license.

I WILL NOT CHANGE

Hardness of heart is basically a stubbornness, insisting on something that does not work. It's what causes husbands to declare that they will not change, even when they see their marriage going down the drain. It's what causes wives to be set in their ways, refusing to listen to the requests their husbands are making of them. If the way you act is not good for your marriage, and you don't want to change, know that you are destined to die alone.

We frequently harden our hearts in self-defence. After being hurt so much, perhaps by some infidelity, lies, harsh words, or other painful experience at the hands of our partners, it's natural for our hearts to become hardened. We become distant and emotionally disconnected as a way of preventing that person from hurting us again. The problem is that building walls to protect our hearts is not wise—unless you want to be trapped inside, alone, with all those bad feelings, like a prisoner in a haunted house. Those who build walls end up building a prison for themselves.

Think about it: if your spouse is truly determined to hurt you and you see no more reason to fight for the marriage, then leave him once and for all. But if you're still willing to try because you believe there's hope, then you have to tear down the walls and soften your heart. If you live with your partner and insist on keeping your walls up, you must really like to suffer. Remember: if your heart remains hardened, not even God can help you.

Examine your heart and see if perhaps it's been hardened by any of these things:

- Pride
- Selfishness
- Being set in your ways
- Always being defensive
- Unbending in your point of view
- Being unforgiving
- A tendency to resist and/or deny physical intimacy
- Inflexibility (unwillingness to change)
- An "I'm never wrong" attitude
- A taker, not a giver
- A tendency to dwell on the past
- A tendency to build walls to keep your partner out
- Insincerity (you hide your feelings)
- Finger-pointing (your partner's flaws)
- An inability to apologize
- Uncaring (about your partner's feelings)
- An unwillingness to listen
- Constantly trying to change your partner
- You've made up your mind about an issue and will not change it (defending your position as the only valid one, of course)
- A habit of emotional blackmail
- A controlling nature

- A "this is the way I am" attitude to excuse any inappropriate behavior
- An inability to admit you need help
- A tendency to use hurtful words
- An emotionally cold and distant nature
- An inability to open up and share your feelings with your partner

Take a look at yourself with these points in mind. Make an honest examination of your heart. Are there any stones that need to be broken? What would your spouse say about you if he or she went through this list? As long as your heart is hardened, you will never be happy in your love life.

Cristiane:

To further complicate this situation, there are two types of hardened hearts: those who are clearly hard of heart, whose attitude is visible to all, and those who see themselves as victims. Both are hardened and very accusatory of their partners.

This is what happened with Renato and me. For the first twelve years of our marriage, I blamed him for not being the husband I needed him to be. His way of attempting to solve our problems was terrible. He would stay angry for days, and in the end I was always the one who had to apologize. I would apologize so that our marriage could move forward, but I wasn't wholehearted about it. I continued to believe that he was the problem, so much so that I was always praying for him (feeling righteous in my own eyes). I felt like an undervalued wife, because I gave so much of myself and hardly got anything back. I even wrote a sad, depressing song for the soundtrack of our "love" story. Then came the phone call from chapter 9. After that I changed a lot. I began focusing on what I could do and discovered that I also had been hard-hearted for all those years. But mine was the victim type.

Yes, Renato should have given me the proper attention as my husband. No, he should not have punished me by not speaking to me for days after I did something he didn't like. But what good is it to know that your spouse is failing in his responsibilities, when you are doing the same?

At first, this revelation scared me. I had always considered myself to be a great wife to Renato. I always gave him my best. How could I have been harsh and mean to him? This is where many get stuck in a vicious cycle of frustration. Love is giving. But when you get to the point that you both stop giving, and each of you is waiting to see who will give first . . . it's over. You will continue going round and round, a real 360° "change"! You will change for a couple of months, but then you go right back to where you started from.

My hard-heartedness insisted that Renato change. I constantly demanded things of him. Whenever I did something for him, I'd sit back and watch for what he was going to do for me. And if I didn't get anything in return, I would go right back to my demanding ways. And you know, there are various ways of being demanding. You can complain, make an ugly face, make a few indirect comments, use emotional blackmail, make comparisons, and so on, and so on. All these attitudes come from the victim type of hard-heartedness.

I believe this is the worst type, because these people cannot see what they're doing. We think we're right. We raise the "how long do I have to be the only one giving?" flag—but what are we accomplishing when we give with our right hand and demand with our left?

I had this kind of hard-heartedness, and that's why our problems lasted as long as they did. I am totally aware of that now. In fact, as soon as I softened my heart, Renato changed, and my marriage was transformed. I had been hindering my prayers and all our attempts to change.

My change was simple. I believe that change is easier for the victim than it is for the defensive person. I simply stopped imposing. I sacrificed what I felt he should do, and I stopped pointing the finger and being so demanding. Simple! That was it. And what did I get in return? We're here writing a book on the subject. Obviously, it was worth it!

Those who give in first will have the privilege of telling others what I am about to tell you right now: I changed first, clearing the way for my husband to change as well. Not everyone is able to do this.

GETTING RID OF THE STONES

If you acknowledge that there are stones and walls in your heart and you want to change, the first step is to get help from the One who hates divorce. Remember Him? Since God hates divorce, we can safely conclude that He also hates the hard-heartedness responsible for so many broken marriages. Clearly, God wants to help you overcome this. Heres what He says:

> *I will give you a new heart and put a new spirit within you; I will take the heart of stone out of your flesh and give you a heart of flesh.* (Ezekiel 36:26)

In order for God to help you, you have to admit to your mistakes. You can start by humbly offering a sincere prayer: "My God, I want a new heart. Take away my heart of stone and give me a heart of flesh. Show me how to behave. Help me to be the person You want me to be."

If you don't agree with what we're saying and would prefer to continue doing things your way, then you can forget it. Not even God can help those who refuse to renounce their heart of stone. But if you sincerely want to surrender and allow God to mold you into the person you need to be, He will help you destroy your heart of stone, restore your marriage, and avoid any possible divorce in the making.

But don't assume that you can now sit idly by while God does all the work. That is not how things work. God requires a partnership before He will act. He's going to help you do what you cannot do, but your effort is necessary. God will give you the tools to destroy your hardened heart. Grinding stones is not an easy job, but we're going to tell you what to do, and not to do, to achieve this.

Recognizing our mistakes is very painful, but this is where you have to start. If you go through the pain now, you will experience relief for the rest of your life. The alternative is to cling to your mistakes and sink with them, suffering for years to come. Which do you prefer?

 ## TASK:

Have a talk with your spouse. Ask him or her this question: what makes me a difficult person to live with? Write down the answers and then switch roles. As you answer the question, your spouse can write down your answers. If your spouse doesn't want to do this exercise, think about the main complaints he or she commonly makes about you, and write them down. Remember: the smartest person takes the first step toward change. Pay attention to the rules: paper, pen, listen, and write. You are not allowed to disagree or defend yourselves. There should be zero emotions during this task. Simply explore the other person's point of view, even if you disagree. The important thing is to understand what he or she is feeling.

Don't take anything personally. Remember to put your emotions on a shelf before starting this task. Even if you do not agree, take a deep breath and continue. Don't attack your partner's character, and try to express yourself in a way that focuses on the problem. Then protect this list with your life. Do not lose it. Show your spouse that you're taking this exercise seriously.

If you put your emotions to the side and remain focused, this list will hold precious information that will be useful in your making changes. This is not a competition. Don't worry about whose list is longer. What matters is that you put everything out on the table. Another crucial point: after this exercise, you should no longer point out these items to your partner, or demand that they work on an item on the list. You are only responsible for what you need to work on.

Roll up your sleeves and pull that hammer out of your tool box. Today you start breaking stones.

/BulletproofMarriage

On our Facebook page
fb.com/BulletproofMarriage
post: *I started breaking the stones in my heart.*
#Bulletproofmarriage

@BulletproofMate

Tweet: *I started breaking the stones in my heart.*
#BulletproofMarriage
@BulletproofMate

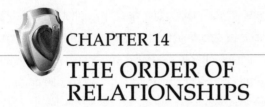

CHAPTER 14

THE ORDER OF RELATIONSHIPS

In school we learn that basic mathematics teaches us that "factors can be multiplied in any order and the product is always the same." This always works in multiplication, but this rule doesn't always apply to our lives. In a marriage, the order of factors changes the final product a great deal. After an Olympic competition, the winners are placed on the podium in winning order and receive awards according to their final positions. No one would give the gold medal to the third-place runner, or bronze to the first-place runner, but you may be doing this at home because you simply do not know who deserves the three positions on your marriage podium.

THIS REFEREE IS NEVER BIASED

God clearly states that He should come first in our lives. This is not egotism on His part. He knows what He's doing. He knows people and realizes that chaos is inevitable when this rule is not followed. When you don't put God in first place, you will naturally occupy that position. And when you put yourself first in life, get ready because no one will be able to put up with you! You'll make all sorts of mistakes and will end up a selfish bore, as we mentioned in the previous chapter. Your heart will harden, and you'll end up letting your marriage go down the drain. God suggests that we put Him in first place so that we have a referee in life. Having a referee is essential, especially in marriage.

Without a doubt, I can say my marriage was saved because we both put God in first place. If it were not for that, I'm not sure we'd still be together. Marriage is the union of two completely different people—so it's only natural that there will be times you disagree, in spite of your love. One will say A, the other will say B, and both will be sure they are right. How can you solve this problem? There is only one solution: have a referee, a judge. His impartial law will make the final decision.

There have been times when I had to back off from my reasoning, as did Cristiane, and allow God's reasoning to prevail. It was no longer what I wanted, what I thought was right, or what she thought was right, but what God said and determined should be done. You can't imagine how much simpler this makes a couple's life; it solves so many problems.

Isn't this what Jesus established when He was asked about the most important commandment of all? *You shall love the Lord your God with all your heart, with all your soul, and with all your mind. This is the first and great commandment. And the second is like it: You shall love your neighbor as yourself.*[12] God first, your neighbour second—in that order. But who is your closest neighbor? Isn't it your husband or wife?

When we worked in Texas, we came across many people who exhibited a shallow spirituality. Many of these people attended our marriage course and got really excited about it. They would tell all their friends about it, and even began to see great changes in their relationship. And yet, in many cases, those changes were not enough to permanently transform their marriages. Although the great majority of the attendees belonged to a church, since most people in Texas are evangelical Christians, they did not have a real relationship with God. There is a big difference. Having a real relationship with God, treating

---

[12] Matthew 22:36-40.

Him like the most important person in our lives and proving it with our attitudes, has nothing to do with religion or religious practices. I like the way my colleague, Marcus Vinícius, explained during one of our courses how couples should look to God:

> *When you look to God, try to remove all religious prejudices. View God as righteousness; see Him as truth. Not your truth, nor your spouse's truth, but the truth that's going to help both of you overcome your problems together. This has nothing to do with religion, but with the important values that every human being needs and appreciates. It is not wise to deny Him first place in your life. If what you think is fair is different from what your partner thinks is fair, whose opinion will prevail in the end? Only the righteousness that comes from above, the perfect righteousness, can bring true balance and justice into your relationship—and without justice there can be no love.*

If you have no higher authority to mediate your conflicts, you will end up stuck in your own opinions. Who's right? She thinks she's right, and he thinks he is, but thinking doesn't necessarily mean or prove anything. That's why every sport has rules and every country has a constitution. You can't show up at work in shorts unless you're a lifeguard. In other words, there has to be discipline or else things will become a mess. Why would it be any different in marriage? You may not like the rules, but they exist to help regulate our relationships with people.

If there were no referees on a football field, the game would never end, no fouls would be called, and confusion would reign. Both teams would want to play until they won and would never agree on anything. Players frequently badmouth referees, but the teams (and fans) understand that they are necessary to maintain order. Likewise, when we place God first in our lives, He becomes the Judge in our marriage. It's well worth having Him around for those times when we're unable to reach an agreement . . . This is when we search for God's view on the situation and then obey His decision with confidence, knowing that it'll be for the best. After all, He is not a biased referee. It's very difficult to have a happy marriage when we ignore the rules of the game as established by God.

AND THE SILVER MEDAL GOES TO . . .

After the gold medal is awarded to God, there you are with a silver medal in your hand . . . You wish you could put it around your own neck, your son's little neck, or your mother's. But the proper answer lies in the Bible passage that cites the creation of marriage. Do you remember this passage?

> *Therefore a man shall leave his father and mother and be joined to his wife, and they shall become one flesh. (Genesis 2:24)*

Marriage came with this little rule in the instruction manual. For man (and woman) to get married, he must first leave his father and mother, leave the nest. If we have to leave our parents, the most influential people in our lives, do we really have to ask about siblings, friends, and our ex-girlfriend's Facebook page? "And they shall become one flesh" indicates the beginning of a new family. When you get married, you leave your family of origin and form a new family. Your new family is your spouse. Your parents, siblings, and other family members become your relatives, as shown in the following diagram.

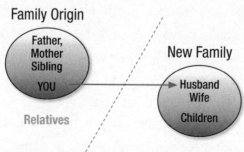

Your original family becomes relatives after marriage

I am not saying that parents and siblings are no longer important, but you need to move to your own nest and start your new family. Clear boundaries are necessary to maintain a healthy relationship with all concerned. If this line is not clear, there will be unwelcome interference.

A common mistake of newlyweds and their relatives is that they're not seen as a separate family until they have a child. When the first child arrives, it's common to hear "Now our family's complete," but that overlooks the fact that the family was complete from the moment they got married. Having children is a choice, not a mandatory step in a relationship. (And please, never make the decision to have a child as a means to solving a problem between you and your spouse, or filling a void. It'll never work.)

Man joins his wife and they become one flesh. A new family is born, completed, and sealed, with no room for interference from third parties. Besides God, nothing and nobody should take precedence over your husband or wife. If you are one flesh, then when you take care of your spouse, you're taking care of your own body. By prioritizing your partner, the most important part of you, you are prioritizing yourself.

Unfortunately, many women think it's this kind of relationship they should have with their children, who are blood of their blood. After you've carried a baby inside your body for nine months, you feel connected to him or her for the rest of their lives—even more than your child's father. But your child who came forth from you will grow up and want to live his own life and form his own family. Becoming one flesh with someone who will inevitably leave your home in a number of years makes no sense. This is a recipe for frustration and suffering. Children need to experience the solid base of their parents' marriage in order to form their own base in the future.

The strength of a relationship is in a couple's bond, and the only way to have a strong bond is by establishing proper priorities. Those who put work above their spouses create a rift in the relationship. And yet the problem that occurs is that it's so easy to let other things or people come before your husband or wife, even when you would not verbally admit it. If anybody asks, you're likely to say that your spouse is more important, but your actions prove who, or what, truly comes first.

The importance we place on a person or thing is measured by the time we devote to it and by what we do, not by what we say. We need to observe our actions. Who has received the most, or better part, of our time, effort, attention, and thoughts? Your spouse should receive preferential treatment and the best of your time. If most of it is spent at your mother's house or with co-workers, you are exposing your marriage to great risk and leaving it without protection. You need to pay close attention to this every single day. Stop and weigh your actions.

I'd say "I love you" to my wife, but the way I ignored and failed to take care of her canceled out my words. My actions proved to her that the most important thing in my life was my job. In my case, it is still a mite tricky because my job is serving God. It's so easy to get confused and assume that if God is in first place, then everything that is related to Him should also be in first place. But don't confuse God with the work of God.

Though I worked as a pastor, and served God, I should not have put the work of God before my wife. He makes this clear when He speaks about pastors, bishops, and every other servant of God, saying that they have to have a good marriage and take care of their families first, so that afterward they can take care of the church. God is not contradicting Himself when He says a pastor should take care of his family first. He will still occupy first place because the work of God is not God. He places great value on marriage! He doesn't want you to do His work if you are not a good example at home or fail to care for your spouse as the first sheep in your flock. In fact, marriage serves as a gauge to measure our relationship with God. If I am close to God, I will do very well in my marriage. If I'm not doing well in my marriage, then my relationship with God will not be good.

For a marriage to work, a husband and wife have to care for each other more than for any other person or thing. If this doesn't happen, there is no real marriage. When a wife occupies the correct spot on the podium, she will feel honored to have been chosen above all other women. If she's pushed off to the side, she'll become a bitter and unhappy woman. An unhappy woman makes for an unhappy home, and let's face it, that is not something you want. When a husband occupies the correct spot, he feels respected for being allowed to care for his wife as if she were his own body.

Now that you know these things and are one flesh, remove anyone else from the equation. The closeness that you have with your spouse should be similar to being glued together, inseparable. There can be no other person between you, not even your children.

Of course, there are rare exceptions. If your husband is a hard-line drug user, his behavior creates risks for the entire family. In this case, you and the children, if you have any, become the priority because your husband's actions put your family's safety at risk. In this case, a temporary separation might be needed so that he can seek treatment. Of course, if God were first in his life, he would not be addicted to a drug, but that's a topic for a whole different book.

With first and second place duly filled by God and your spouse, third place goes to the rest of humanity: children, relatives, friends, and other people. Let's get organized.

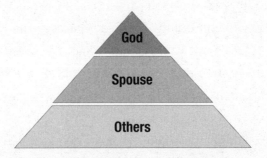

The order of relationships as determined by God.

WHAT TO DO ABOUT NOSY PEOPLE?

It's not easy to draw the line with friends and relatives, especially when they have already had a habit of intruding before you got married. But before you start complaining about your family, stop inviting the intrusions. When you share your problems with friends and relatives, you're giving them permission to judge your spouse, make biased judgments, and treat your life as if it were theirs. If you expose your life to your relatives as though it were a soap opera, you can't complain afterward.

What should you do when nosy relatives invade your relationship? Fighting and throwing a fit are useless. Use your head. When people from your spouse's family of origin are the invaders, understand that relatives will always be relatives. It's not smart to attack them because you'll be attacking your partner's origins and creating an even bigger problem. Then they will see *you* as the invader who is trying to break them apart. The ideal thing to do is treat them the best you can and work on winning them over.

Deal with evil at its roots and don't take things personally. For example, often the root behind a mother-in-law's bickering with her son's wife is because of her own insecurity. If you treat your mother-in-law well, clearly communicate that you are not her rival, and that your goal is to make her son the happiest man in the world, you will make her feel more secure and less prone to give you problems. She should view you as her ally, someone to love and respect, never as an enemy. Learn to love your mother-in-law, even if it feels like Mission Impossible at the moment. If you've come this far in this book, you know it's not impossible. Remember Dian Fossey and the gorillas?

If it's relatives from your family of origin who often like to interfere in your marriage, then learn to prioritize your new family and show it by your attitudes. Be polite, don't intentionally hurt anyone, but establish clear boundaries so that relatives get the message that your family is sacred ground. Let them know that when they criticize your spouse, they're criticizing you. Whoever loves you will have to learn to love your spouse as well, because the two of you are now one.

When a couple decides to help a relative with financial problems, there is great potential for creating conflict. And yet, if you discuss things beforehand and reach an agreement, then normally there's no problem. Couples need to be balanced and prioritize their needs so that when the occasion arises they can help those in need.

We know a couple who went through serious financial problems. They got into debt early in their marriage. Three years into the marriage, they were struggling to pay off the debt. At the time, the wife was concerned about her mother, who was overdue on some of her bills, and had an emotional talk with her husband and got him to take out a loan to help her. She had already decided the matter before speaking to her husband and would not consider any alternatives . . . relying on some good old emotional blackmail. With no room to maneuver, the husband gave in. And so, her attitude not only increased their debt load, but it also caused wear and tear on their relationship. The husband felt less of a husband when he saw how little his wife prioritized the needs of their new family, nor took into consideration his efforts to paying off their own debt.

Many couples do the right thing in the wrong order. It's not wrong to help your family of origin, as long as it's done at the right time and in the right way, and as long as you're not inconsiderate of your partner. If it makes your partner feel uncomfortable, you'll only create more problems.

Cristiane:
I'll never forget what my father said to me at the altar during my wedding ceremony: "From now on no more running to Mom and Dad. Your problems will have to be resolved between you and Renato."

Out of all he said that night, this is what most impressed me. I think it was because I was still very young and very attached to my family.

His hard, direct words caused me to think about the new order of priorities I now had because of marriage. Renato was my family now, and I was his. Our parents became our relatives. The problems we had in the beginning of our marriage stayed just between us. This isn't easy, especially for us women, who tend to want to say what we feel . . .

It's not hard to understand the concept of how we have to let go of our old family when we start a new one; but even so, this is a major problem among many couples today. This wasn't the case many years ago. The goal of marriage was to form a family. In fact, unmarried women were looked down upon by society and their own families.

At the time, many people got married, even though they had no feelings for each other. It was their duty to get married, and that was it. You didn't always love the person you were marrying. But many couples who got married without feelings for each other developed true love over time because they decided that they were now a family and they should start acting like one. In other words, act like a person who loves your husband or wife, and you will become a couple. And if a couple puts each other first, they'll be a family, and no one will be able to come between them and separate them.

TASK:

What adjustments do you need to make to establish the correct order in your relationship? Write down what you will do, especially what you will do differently, to make your spouse feel like the most important person in the world for you, after God.

 /BulletproofMarriage

On our Facebook page
fb.com/BulletproofMarriage
post: *I just corrected the order of my relationships. #Bulletproofmarriage*

 @BulletproofMate

Tweet: *I just corrected the order of my relationships. #BulletproofMarriage @BulletproofMate*

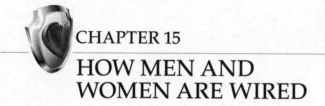

CHAPTER 15

HOW MEN AND WOMEN ARE WIRED

Before beginning this chapter, I did some quick research into how men's minds function differently from women's minds. I stopped writing for a minute, left my office, and went into the bathroom where Cristiane was blow-drying her beautiful hair while listening to music on her iPad. Without letting her know what I was doing, I walked over to the sink and washed my hands. I looked at her in the mirror and asked: what are you thinking about?"

With no hesitation whatsoever, she replied: "I'm thinking about how Rafaela hasn't posted the movie review from last week on my blog yet. I have to send her an e-mail. I was also thinking about how this would be a good song to use on The Love School TV program, but there's probably no official video of it on YouTube, since it's such an old song. But I was thinking . . . production could probably use behind-the-scenes footage from the show to make a clip for this song. And . . . talking about the production team, when I went into their room yesterday, I noticed they need more chairs. It seems that someone always has to work standing up. Oh, and I was also thinking about how dry my hair is. I'd like to pay someone to blow-dry my hair instead of doing it myself."

"Anything else?" I dared ask.

"No, that's all."

That's all . . . my wife had been thinking about five different things, and that song hadn't even finished playing. I was only thinking about one thing: how am I going to write this chapter!

One fact that most couples ignore is the difference between the sexes and how it affects their relationship. Men deal with their wives as if they were dealing with another man. Women speak to their husbands as if they were women. Every one of these interactions opens up a new can of worms.

When you understand these differences, everything changes without anything actually changing. Things change because you begin to understand that your spouse is not doing this or that because he's a bad person or because she wants to irritate you. They're just being who they are: a man or a woman. They're not mean; you're just very different from each other.

Cristiane:

"If I were in his shoes, I wouldn't have done that." This is what I occasionally thought about Renato. I was constantly criticizing men when they showed a lack of sensitivity to others. I would walk into a building carrying a bunch of bags, one heavier than the other, and men would just stand there and not even think of helping me. And I'd think, *I wish men would act more like gentlemen!*

I was constantly comparing myself to Renato, and because we were two very different people, you can just imagine the thoughts that ran through my mind. He didn't even notice my new clothes, whereas my girlfriends noticed them right away. "How can you do that?" I would ask, but he couldn't understand why these things were so important to me. It was as though we were from two different planets! Then one day, I realized I was being unfair by wanting him to think like me. After all, he's a man.

This is a terrible mistake that many of us make. We want other people to think like us. This happens even with things that have to do with taste. When someone likes something different, we think it's horrible, but does it really matter? Does it matter whether or not I like another woman's hair color when her hair is not mine? But this is what we do with our spouses. We criticize them for not always thinking or doing things our way.

In this kind of battle, even in the best of scenarios, nobody wins. On the other hand, it fills a marriage with friction. I wanted him to show the same consideration to me that I showed to him, and he wanted me to be just as tough as he was to put up with things. He wanted me to be a man, and I wanted him to be a woman.

Of course, at first we didn't notice that. I never imagined that I would ever ask my husband to be a woman! But if I had made a list of everything I wanted him to be, it would have been a male version of me. As if I would ever put up with myself!

This is the pure, unadulterated truth. Ask any woman to describe her "ideal man" and she'll describe another woman . . .

But men and women differ in many ways. Genetically, the twenty–third chromosome determines a person's gender. Physically, male and female bodies are obviously different. But one of the most distinct differences is in their brains.

On average, a male brain is 10% larger than a female brain and has 4% more cells. But before the men start bragging about having larger brains, research also shows that female brains have more nerve cells and connectors, which allow the brain to be more efficient and effective. What this means is that, in general, men tend to perform tasks that use the left side of the brain, which is the logical, rational side. Women, on the other hand, tend to use both sides simultaneously because of their ability to rapidly transfer information between left and right sides of the brain. The result is that men tend to be more focused on things, systems, and solving problems, while women tend to be creative and more attuned to how everyone around them is feeling. Studies acknowledge that there are some exceptions, and that it is possible for a man to have a "more feminine" brain and vice versa—which has nothing to do with their sexual preference. Don't worry! This simply means that some men are more emotional and some women are more rational—but they are not the majority.

In Louann Brizendine's book *The Female Brain*, she explains how both brains are already very different from the crib. Baby girls grow into little girls who love to make friends and socialize with other girls. They even notice when things are not going well at home. But when it comes to baby boys, who grow into big boys, things are not the same. They want to play, and if they hurt someone in the process, that's okay, no problem. They love challenge and adventure. At a very young age, he is already a conqueror, and she is already a loving companion.

ONE BOX FOR EACH AND EVERY THING

In my opinion, Mark Gungor spells out these differences the best. He explains that the male brain is made up of boxes. In a man's brain there's a box for everything: one for his car, one for his job, one for you, one for his children, one for his mother-in-law somewhere in the basement, sealed and labeled "Danger! Do not touch" . . . And one very important detail is that these boxes never touch one another. Whenever a man wants to discuss a subject, he pulls out the one box that has to do with that particular topic, opens it, and discusses only what's inside that box. When he's done, he closes the box and puts it back in its place very carefully so that it does not touch any other box.

And there's more: women, pay close attention!

Inside a man's brain there is a little box that most women are unaware of. This box has nothing in it. In fact, it's called "the nothing box." Out of all of the boxes, this little box is his favorite. Whenever he has a chance, he'll run to his nothing box every time. This is why men are able to engage in activities that require virtually zero brain activity for hours on end, such as playing video games, fishing, or sitting in front of the TV surfing channels, though not actually watching anything. If you let us, when we're stressed out or under pressure, we'll automatically gravitate to our little nothing box.

Women have a hard time understanding this because they just can't stop thinking about things. Whenever a woman sees her husband in this vegetative, zombie-like state, she can't help but come over and ask:

"What are you thinking about?"

And with a blank look on his face, he'll answer, "Nothing."

"You must be thinking about *something*. It's impossible to think about nothing."

"I already told you, I wasn't thinking about anything," he insists in vain.

"No, you're lying. You just don't want to tell me. Why won't you tell me?"

Every man has had this conversation and fears it because he knows it's not going to end well. No matter what he says, she's not going to believe him. If he says he wasn't thinking about anything, she doesn't believe that's humanly possible. If he pretends he was thinking about something just to get her off his back, she's going to suspect that he's not being totally honest with her (not realizing that she's hit the nail on the head . . . he really wasn't thinking about that).

What she does not understand is that when men are stressed out, or under pressure at work, their way of relaxing is to run to their little nothing box. He wants to be left alone. He doesn't want to speak. He just wants to be quiet for a while. The last thing he wants to do is talk about his problems and frustrations. A man will only tell another man his problems when he thinks that man can help him solve them. Otherwise, he just keeps trying to process things quietly inside his head. But when a woman is stressed out, she has to speak to someone—not necessarily for advice—because she will literally explode if she doesn't talk about things . . .

A BALL OF WIRES

If a man's brain is made up of a bunch of little boxes, a woman's brain is like a ball of yarn, a tangled web of wires. Everything is connected to everything else: the car is connected to her job, which is connected to her children, who are connected to her mother, who is connected to the leak in the bathroom . . . Everything's tied together and nothing happens by chance. And emotion is the energy flowing through these wires. That's why a woman tends to remember everything, such as the details of a conversation her husband swears never happened. That's because whenever you link an event to an emotion, that event will be burned into your memory and you'll never forget it. Men also have this ability, but the truth is they just don't use it that often because they couldn't care less about the small details. But women remember every single little thing . . .

When a woman is stressed out and needs someone to talk to, the man will mistakenly think he has to solve her problems for her. She might say:

"You know what happened today? Pamela took all the credit for the work I did."

"Who's Pamela?" he asks, completely disengaged from what's going on.

"Honey, she's one of my co-workers at the office!" she tells him for the twentieth time, and continues, "When she handed our boss the project I killed myself to finish these last two weeks, he signed it and assumed she'd done it all on her own."

"Well, you have to tell her that she can't do that. Or find a way to let your boss know that you were the one who put the whole thing together. If not, then just forget it and don't get upset over it."

Her husband thinks he's just solved things by giving her some great advice. The truth is he's just made her feel like an idiot, as though she has no idea what to do in this situation. She doesn't need advice. All she wants is someone to listen to her. She needs to talk because her mind is being bombarded by frustration and with this and that thought. What her husband needs to do right away is shut his mouth and listen. If he doesn't have the sense and self-control to do this, she's going to go to her mother, sister, friend, or even worse, to Richard at the office. If a woman understands her husband's brain and he understands hers, the two can make allowances for these male-female differences, and they will avoid irritating and frustrating each other.

IS HE DEAF?

Because of their differences, women tend to be great multi-taskers and naturally find themselves doing a number of things at the same time. Men tend to be great single-taskers and like to concentrate on one thing at a time. Once again, this can be a source of annoyance. Women often blame men for not paying attention to what they say. For example, a husband may be on the sofa reading the newspaper while the wife is preparing dinner, keeping track of their son while he does his chores, and talking on the phone, all at the same time. She hangs up and says to her husband, "My niece's birthday party is this coming Saturday. We have to be there around three o'clock." He mumbles from the living room, "Yeah, okay."

Fast forward to Saturday, and he notices his wife getting ready for something, and asks, "Where are you going?" She answers in frustration, "You always forget about everything, don't you? You never pay attention to what I say." The reality is that he was totally focused on

173

reading his newspaper when she told him about it. This doesn't mean that he doesn't care about her. It's simply the way his brain works. If you want to reduce these types of misunderstandings, make sure your husband is completely focused on you when you talk to him. In other words, make sure he's looking straight at you and not doing anything else. If not, then wait for the right moment to tell him.

The differences between the sexes dictate much more than a few little rules of coexistence and communication. Over the centuries, men and women have been naturally programmed to expect very specific things from each other. Unfortunately, today more than ever, these expectations are not always clearly understood. We will now attempt to explain how they developed, what they are, and how to satisfy them.

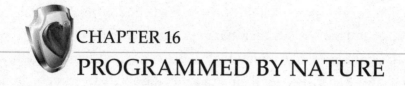

CHAPTER 16
PROGRAMMED BY NATURE

From the very beginning of time, the physical, genetic, and mental makeup of men and women created social and cultural differences, among others. A man's physical strength, skill with weapons, navigating abilities, and competitive nature made him a natural provider and protector of the family. The inherent characteristics of a woman made her a natural carer for the children and home organizer.

Since the beginning, and for thousands of years, their roles have been different, yet clear and specific. The routine of a typical couple was pretty much like what I describe below.

Before sunrise, a man would leave his house with weapons slung over his shoulder to hunt alone, or in a group, and risk his life to bring food back home. A woman stayed home, waiting anxiously for his return at the end of the day, not only with food, but unharmed. He was her hero, who risked his life for her and their children. While hunting, men did not make great use of their verbal skills because any small sound could scare the game away. They had to speak in hushed tones and at times communicate with gestures. They could not be afraid to kill—wild beasts or other men—if they were attacked.

On the other hand, a woman stayed home with her children and neighbors, forcing her to develop better communication skills. As the organizer and nurse of the family, she developed an expertise at noticing details and facial expressions, always alert to the physical and emotional state of others. She became an architect of relationships, the glue that held her family and community together.

You may now understand why men developed an unemotional disposition, are not as good at the inborn female gift of "reading people's moods," and are less talkative and more direct with their words.

In addition to the things they did to hold the home together, women were cherished for their almost divine ability to bear children. She carried within her body the seed of life. For this reason, a man protected and valued her. She, in turn, respected him as the natural leader of the family and appreciated him for risking his life on a daily basis to guarantee the family's survival.

Because of all these things, men and women's roles were clearly defined. There was no argument nor competition. Each knew his or her role in life, and neither was tempted to think they were better than their spouse. It remained this way for thousands of years. Through many centuries these roles hardly varied at all. Men have traditionally been the providers and protectors of the family, and women have been the caregivers of the home and the architects of the marriage relationship.

However, over the past fifty years, certain factors have been gradually causing this reality to change. We could cite many, but we will limit ourselves to only two major factors and their effects on marriage.

THE CONFUSING OF ROLES

Two social phenomena have transformed the traditional concept of a man's and woman's role in society: the Feminist Movement and the Industrial Revolution. It is beyond the scope of this book to go into detail about these two points. Feel free to do your own research if you feel the need. But for our purposes, here are the main points and why we care:

The Industrial Revolution

Women started to leave the home for work, although cautiously at first, in the mid-nineteenth century. Changes in manufacturing and technology gave rise to the opening of factories, which led to job opportunities that had been nonexistent for women up to that point. But over the last century, especially after World War II, women began to make a name for themselves in the job market. They proved themselves to be as capable as men in many professions. They earned equal rights and surpassed men in the number of students enrolled in universities. With the explosive growth in industry, technology, public service, and health care, women are now an essential part of the global economy. With the added buying power of a woman, couples are able to afford much more than their parents and grandparents could. On top of that, the current materialistic culture—relentless advertising of products and goods that promise "happiness" to those who consume them—makes it practically impossible for a man of average or low income to support a family without his wife's extra income. What this means is this: a woman is no longer simply the mother and wife who runs the household and welcomes her husband at the end of the day with a warm cake waiting in the oven. She is as equally busy as her husband and earns as much or more than he does; and so she is strikingly different from a traditional woman. She has also become a hunter.

The Feminist Movement

American feminist and social activist bell hooks[13] defines the essence of feminism as: "Feminism is the struggle to end sexist oppression." I think everyone would agree that throughout history, men have done a great disfavor, not only to women, but also to the

---

[13] She intentionally does not capitalize her name. Curiously, at age sixty she still remains unmarried.

entire masculine gender. And so, the validity of the struggle for women's rights has undeniable value. But just as feminists have made great strides in gender equality, they have also engendered a certain hatred or dislike for men. In general, feminism encourages women to view men as oppressors, as an enemy who's ready to oppress them the first chance he gets. Though this is true in some cases, this generalization leads women to reject the traditional role of men as breadwinners and protectors, for fear that it would be an acknowledgment that they are beneath men. Waving the women's rights flag also creates confusion between equal rights and gender equality. It's when women view men as their equals in terms of gender that numerous conflicts arise, especially in marriage.

I'd like to be very clear about this: I am completely in favor of equal rights for both sexes. But when we say that men and women have the same nature and needs, we make a grave mistake that will have serious consequences in people's love lives. It's one thing to have equal rights, and another to assume you have the same roles. Men and women have always had equal rights in God's eyes, since He didn't create one to be better than the other. But the roles they were assigned are altogether different. The problem begins when a woman wants to fulfil a man's role in a marriage and family.

These two factors can be summarized in one phrase: the rise of women. As a result, their roles are no longer as clear, distinct, and specific as they used to be. For the first time in human history, men are beginning to experience an identity crisis.

WHO AM I? WHERE AM I?

Who's this female "hunter" at my side? Men haven't adjusted to this new scenario, and the changes we have just discussed are precisely what are behind a large number of marriage problems. Women have become more independent, and as a result, they are less likely to involve husbands in their decisions. They butt heads because they feel they "can" do this or that on their own. Men in turn feel intimidated by the growth in women's power, and so they withdraw. In some cases, men start to feel less than women. His traditional firmness turns to indecision, and he does whatever it takes to please his wife and keep the peace. She in turn gets frustrated with his lack of initiative and ends up taking the lead. This vicious cycle continues, and in the end, she takes on his role and he takes on hers.

The result of all this can be seen in the parallel that exists between the rise in feminism over the last fifty years and the huge increase in the number of divorces. How can something so good for women be so bad for our relationships?

We are not suggesting that the advancements that women have made are bad, and we do not want society to go back to the way it used to be. We just want to highlight the fact that though society has changed, the basic needs of men and women have remained the same for thousands and thousands of years. Men are still men and women have not stopped being women. We were created this way. New rights and norms are not going to change our DNA. We are naturally programmed to be this way—we are made to expect certain things from our spouses.

Men and women can grow and evolve as much as they want. There is no inherent problem in a woman earning more money than a man, or in a man washing dishes or helping to change diapers. What both sexes need to understand is *how to meet each other's basic needs*. Let's hold on to the progress and advancements of women, but at the same time rescue the original values and principles that make for a happy marriage.

Cristiane:

I'm in favor of women's rights. I, too, like to achieve big things. The problem is knowing how to act toward our men when it comes to all these changes in society.

My parents have been married for more than forty years, and their mindset is very different from the couples who get married today. When my father married my mother, he thought about working hard to support her. Today, many men no longer have that concern. Women also work and often may even support their husbands. In the past, this would have been humiliating for a man because it made him look weak. If he took a girl from her parents' home, he had an obligation to care of her and provide everything she would ever need.

Meanwhile, her duty was to take care of her husband, their home, and raise their children. She took pleasure in doing this, which is something we do not often see these days. Modern women do not always find pleasure in caring for their husbands, let alone the house. If he's hungry, he can cook himself something to eat. Her children spend most of their time in school and sports, so she has more time for her career and other interests. When she arrives home, she doesn't want to have the hassle of cooking or cleaning anything, so she gets upset when her husband leaves a pair of shoes in the middle of the room. What was not a problem in the past has now become the cause of an argument.

Men and women were not made to compete with each other. We are very different, and our differences were meant to improve our spouse's life, not to be used as ammunition to make it worse for them.

The media contributes to this disaster by helping to put men down. Have you ever noticed that most comedies and other types of movies cast men as the weaker characters, who are afraid of women, do everything wrong, have no say and inspire no confidence—while women are intelligent, know what they want, do everything right, and support the family?

This distorted image of man ends up brainwashing people into thinking: men are weak, women are strong, men are fools, women are smart. The result is that children no longer respect their fathers, wives don't respect their husbands, and men end up abandoning the family. Wives are quick to accuse men of being incapable of supporting the family, and children feel disappointed in their fathers, and tell themselves that they'll never get married.

We've just painted you the picture of a family in the twenty-first century. If society does not value a man's role in the family, men will not value a woman's role, and what happens next is inevitable: no one appreciates anyone else, it's every person for himself or herself—and overblown selfishness every day of their lives.

If you want to have a happy, long-lasting marriage, you cannot follow the rules of today's culture. You must swim against the current and create your own culture within your marriage. Cristiane and I have our own culture, and we've determined that nothing harmful will be allowed to enter. This is why we are able to maintain values and principles that we need to protect our closeness—and we do not forget to fulfill each other's basic needs, which are predetermined by our different natures.

Do you know what these needs are? Let's understand a little bit more about them.

BASIC PREDETERMINED NEEDS

We are programmed by human nature to have certain needs that have to be met. The most basic are food, water, clothing, and shelter. Deprive a man of these things, and he will start behaving like an animal. This can be seen when natural disasters strike a city. All of a sudden, people find themselves without food, water, shelter, and safety. If emergency services do not respond quickly and help these people, they switch into survival mode and become aggressive. The desperate search for food, water, and shelter can cause people to act

181

like cavemen. When people are deprived of their basic needs, they react in primitive ways.

Minutes before a disaster occurs, most people are concerned with insignificant things: is one pant leg shorter than the other, should I paint my bedroom beige or white, should I upgrade my phone? etc. After a horrible tragedy, nobody cares about those things. They're concerned about saving their lives. What they saw as a "necessity" a few minutes ago is now insignificant compared to basic things such as water, food, and blankets. People who've never stolen a thing, never attacked anyone or broken the law, are now capable of doing those very things. It's instinctual for a human being. So then, how can we best contain this animalistic behavior? By fulfilling their basic needs.

There is something else that's important to know:

You can't question a person's basic needs. The only thing you can do is meet them.

It's not a crime to be hungry. You're not an evil person for wanting a good night's sleep. Being thirsty is not against the law. No one should be made to feel guilty for wanting a proper home. People who could meet these needs and don't are the ones who are evil.

Now, apply this logic to your relationship. Men and women also have basic needs that need to be met, because of their male and female makeup. Certain basic things need to be done for a marriage to work. Okay, your husband may not be as romantic as Robert Redford, your wife may not be the image of perfection from the latest Hollywood hit— and yet, you should provide the essentials to each other, at the very least.

The basic needs of a man and woman are extremely important. If they're not met, your husband or wife will begin to act irrationally. And at that point it's useless to criticize or wonder "Why is he like that?" or "Why is she acting that way?" The best thing you can do about your partner's basic needs is meet them. There's no discussing a person's needs. When you're starving, the only helpful thing you can do is eat.

When you buy a pet, the first thing you do is find out what it eats, drinks, likes, and dislikes—even before you take it home. You don't argue with the salesman or try to change the animal's eating habits. If you want a happy pet, all you have to do is meet its needs, no matter how much work you have to put into that. If you want a happy husband or wife, find out what his or her basic needs are and meet them. Don't argue about them, just meet them.

WANTS AND COMPARISONS

A clarification: we're talking about basic needs, not wants, whims, or dreams. A warning for women: true love is not about romance and Hollywood kisses. Women often make the big mistake of comparing real men to men in movies. A married woman once left a comment on one of our YouTube videos describing her ideal man:

> . . .*I like a man that takes care of himself, knows how to express his feelings, and is romantic like Brad Pitt or Tom Cruise. But he has to be a gentleman like James Bond and a provider and protector like Conan the Barbarian or the men from the Wild West. I think the ideal man is like that vampire from Twilight. And I also like that man from* Gone with the Wind, *and the one from* Dancing in the Rain . . . *Oh, I don't know, maybe a little bit of each one. I also like the* Samurais . . .

My first advice for this wife was pretty simple: stop watching movies!

If you don't know what you want, how can you expect your husband to know? The illusion of love that Hollywood creates causes lots of marriages to fail. That kind of love that is scripted and practised with a producer directing the actor doesn't exist in real life. In real life, that soap opera hunk has been married three or four times, has an unhappy love life, and may even beat his wife. We can't live out reality based on fantasy.

One of the worst things you can do is compare your spouse to someone else, anyone—real or imaginary. This will kill your marriage. If you compare your husband to TV husbands, get ready for frustration.

The same applies to men. The same thing will happen when you drift off into the plague of *pornography*. Putting aside the moral aspect of this subject, the fact is that many men are no longer sexually excited by their wives as a result of this addiction. They only find "pleasure" in porn and masturbation. Real life intimacy with his wife no longer is enough. These men stop being the men their wives need, experience frustration from comparing their wives to the women on the videos they watch, and find themselves living in a fantasy world, thus creating an expiration date for their marriages.

No woman likes to be compared in this way. It's humiliating for her to know that her husband is only satisfied by these types of images. In the end, she no longer gets as excited as him, and both are robbed of achieving total intimacy. A man who depends on this kind of stimulation demoralizes his wife and sends her the clear message that she is not enough for him—which is exactly the opposite of her most basic need.

PART IV

BULLETPROOFING IT

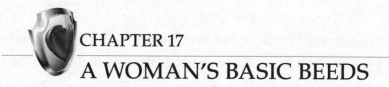

CHAPTER 17
A WOMAN'S BASIC BEEDS

What are the basic needs of a woman? We can sum it up in one sentence: to be valued and cared for. This is how spiritual wisdom defines a husband's primary responsibility to his wife:

> *Husbands, go all out in your love for your wives, exactly as Christ did for the church—a love marked by giving, not getting . . . And that is how husbands ought to love their wives. They're really doing themselves a favor—since they're already "one" in marriage.* (Ephesians 5.25, 28, MSG)

Notice the comparison in the very beginning of this passage between a husband's love for his wife and Christ's love for the Church. God's love is used as an example to be followed. The love we have for our wives should not be modeled after movies, books, parents, relatives, or friends. The Author of marriage pointed to the love of Jesus as a reference point for husbands. And what kind of love did He have? A love marked by selfless giving, sacrifice, care, and renunciation—not emotion.

Men are then led to understand that loving their wives is the same as loving themselves. When I take care of Cristiane, I am actually taking care of myself. If I were to hurt her, I would be hurting myself. Do you remember that the two people in marriage "become one flesh"? Husbands should see their wives as an extension of themselves and refuse to neglect their needs.

A wife is a gift from God to her husband.[14] God created women for men, and the way men were made also complements women. If a husband rejects, mistreats, or abandons his wife, he is rejecting God's gift (the same is true for a wife who rejects her husband). When you belittle your wife by saying "women just want to spend money," or when you belittle your husband by saying "men are all the same," you are actually belittling God because He created both.

A wife is under her husband's care. The origin of the word *husband* stems from a word that means "tiller of the ground." This image of what a husband is fits well with his role and invokes the idea of caring for, helping to grow. So when a man gets married he becomes the one who is to be responsible for his wife, for everything that happens to her, and for caring for her. This is true love. Love is much more than a feeling. It is action. The world says: "If you no longer have feelings for each other, you no longer love each other." This feeling-based love generates serial daters—they simply stop loving one person and go on to the next, and then the next, etc. True love is not based on emotion, but on the care that a husband has for his wife and the commitment he has made to her.

APPRECIATE AND LOVE HER. BUT HOW?

A wife feels appreciated and loved when:

Her husband makes her feel secure—This is not simple physical and financial security, but *security* in every sense of the word. The dictionary defines secure as:

---

14 Proverbs 18:22.

Not subject to threat; certain to remain or continue safe and unharmed; protected against attack; feeling safe, stable, and free from fear or anxiety.[15]

A man can make a woman feel secure in several ways. One way is to be faithful to her. A basic need of a woman is to know that her husband will stay faithful to her when he goes to work or anywhere else. When a man flirts with other women, even when it's a result of his outgoing personality, he makes his wife feel insecure. His playful behavior, which may invite inappropriate friendships with other women, may need to be toned down so that his wife can feel more secure (a wife's jealously, at times, is the result of her husband not providing a sense of security). Being irresponsible, immature, indecisive, strong tempered, a big spender, or given to addictions will also make her feel insecure. Men want their wives to trust them, but their behavior may be sending the wrong message. A man may think that being loud, screaming, and slamming doors proves that he's strong and decisive, and yet he's actually proving the complete opposite. If he can't control himself, how will he control his family or the situation? Show me an angry, volatile husband, and I'll show you an insecure, undervalued, unloved wife.

When a woman feels unsafe, she erects walls to protect herself from whatever that insecurity may bring her way. Her instincts tell her that she has to protect herself, since her husband's not going to do it. This also creates a vicious cycle where he feels disrespected and backs away, and then she feels obligated to make decisions, take initiative, and fight for herself—all of which increases his feelings that she is disrespecting him.

A husband has to be balanced and confident in himself. To protect and care for his wife, he has to be strong, but in the right way. He can't

---

[15] Oxford Online Dictionary.

be an addict nor can he be indecisive. He can't want something one minute and something else the next. If he's immature, irresponsible, and has no strong leadership skills, it's a sure thing that she will take the lead to ensure her own survival . . . Men, it's time to wake up!

He listens to her—This is difficult for a man, because men usually find it a challenge to pay attention for long periods of time or listen to details. They prefer to solve problems rather than hear about them, which is what a woman normally does when she is with her friends. A woman already feels better just by venting to her girlfriend. So you have another problem: you want your wife to share everything with you, but you really don't want to listen to her. No wonder women confide in their friends more often than in their own husbands!

Husbands frequently get angry with their wives when they find out that they have shared something private with another person. But what can she do when her husband doesn't care to hear what she has to say? She's wrong . . . but so is he. If no one listens to her at home, there's a great chance that she will open up to someone willing to listen outside the home. This represents a serious danger. When a woman's basic needs are neglected, she's an easy target for a friendly, helpful Casanova at work who can spot a woman with unmet needs a mile away, and who gives married women what their husbands have no time to give: a listening ear. When these women aren't given the attention they need at home, they become easy candidates for emotional affairs.

Men: open your ears. Pay attention to them, don't ignore them, especially when they're opening up about their problems. Don't try to fix them, just listen. As we previously explained, women handle stress differently from men. They have to talk and release all that's disturbing them inside. This does not mean that she needs your advice. Probably all she needs is to be reassured that you're on her side with listening ears and some hugs.

A couple's intimacy begins when they listen to each other. If you have no conversations, intimacy levels are most probably very low, because it's not only about the physical act of sex. Intimacy goes far beyond just sex. One more tip for men: stop what you're doing and pay attention when she's talking, and you'll avoid problems later on! Worse than not listening is to pretend that you're listening . . . If you are unable to pay attention at that moment, let her know, or else you'll run into problems later on.

I had to learn how to listen. I didn't like to listen or explain details. When my wife asked, "How was your day?" the most I would say was, "It was good." That would be the end of the conversation. But this was destroying our intimacy. So I began to involve her in my life and make her feel that she was a part of my day.

He makes her feel she's the only one—She has a need to feel that out of all the women in the world she's the only one you care about romantically. And that she's the only one for you. You could have chosen any other woman, but you chose her. She comes before your mother, children, siblings, and friends. If someone in your family doesn't like your wife, you should be ready to walk into that relative's house holding her hand, proving that she's important to you and that you'll defend her at all costs. If there's a woman at your job or in your circle of friends who makes your wife feel insecure, it's your responsibility to make her feel secure with your actions (not only your words). I know a husband who does this by practicing a simple rule of thumb: not giving any woman a ride home, out of respect for his wife. Imagine how this makes her feel? She must feel like the woman in this beautiful love letter, written by Graciliano Ramos to his future wife:

I have noticed a strange phenomenon lately: the women died. I think there was an epidemic among them. After December they began disappearing,

191

disappearing, and now there is not one left. True, I see people wearing skirts out there, but I'm not sure if they are women . . . They all died. And this is why I am so drawn to the sole survivor. (Love letters to Heloise)

A woman needs to feel she's the only one. She tends to be insecure by nature. Society adds to this by bombarding her with images of what it deems beautiful and ugly in a woman, always comparing her to its standards: the ideal body, hair, skin, and stylish clothes. You don't see the same attack on men because they usually don't care about their looks as women do. If a friend tells him he's developing a spare tire, they'll laugh about it together; if a friend said the same thing to her, that person would immediately be added to her blacklist . . .

This is why a woman never tires of asking her husband whether or not he thinks she's pretty or loves her. Men who don't understand the reasoning behind this are tempted to say something like: "I proved that I love you when I married you. If anything changes, I'll let you know." It seems obvious to you, but it is not that simple for her. Be careful how you talk to your wife, because this can also contribute to her insecurity.

She's always on your radar—A wife should always be on her husband's radar. He should always be conscious of how and where she is, who she's with, what her present concerns are, and what she's doing or needs. His radar is usually directed at work, bills, his own projects and concerns. But even when his focus is on these things, from time to time he has to remember her and point his radar in her direction.

If you forget to think about her throughout the day, you will probably be greeted with an angry face when you arrive home. As her protector, you have to be aware of her every step, not because you want to spy on or control her, but because you want to fulfil your role as a good caretaker.

Many couples are heading for divorce because they've turned their radar away from each other. They no longer care about what the other does or where the other goes. They are indifferent toward each other. This is how love grows cold. Every relationship needs constant investment. If he forgets about her because of a job or a new project, she will feel unappreciated and unloved. Many women live in jealousy not because their husbands cheat on them. The root cause is because their husband has not made her feel appreciated.

When she gets sick, he expects her mother or friends to take care of her, when he is the one who should do that whenever possible. If she's starting a new project, it's his responsibility to find out how these projects are going. She's his responsibility. He cannot brush her to the side as if she were any other woman in the world.

A wife once told us that her husband never had time for her because of his job. So, with his consent, she decided to schedule a vacation three months in advance for them to go on. The week before the vacation he told her he wouldn't be able to go because of his job and that she'd have to go with a friend and their children. How do you think she felt when her husband put his job ahead of her?

He makes her feel attractive—When a woman asks the question that every man dreads: "Do you think I'm fat?"—and she really is a bit overweight, you can't lie, but you have to be diplomatic . . . Women need to feel attractive because they're up against a lot of competition: magazines, newspapers, TV, women on the streets. . . The pressure is so intense that even models, the standards of beauty, often feel ugly. This need has been with her since her childhood. Girls love compliments, while boys don't really care. A woman needs praise. Don't be stingy with it.

A man should use words that make her feel like a woman. When she feels ugly, her self-esteem is low and that's bad for both. When Cristiane puts on a few extra pounds, she asks me what I think, and

I always say, "That's great. Now there's a little more of you for me to love!"

There will always be a better-looking woman. There will never be a woman unanimously voted the most beautiful in the world. That's impossible. Beauty is very subjective. But in a husband's eyes his wife has to be the most beautiful woman in the world. He should only have eyes for her.

A husband needs to learn how to be his wife's lover, to see beyond her flaws. When he does this, his wife may be considered "ugly" by society, but she'll feel like the sexiest woman in the world because of how her husband makes her feel. A wise man will make his wife feel attractive.

He is affectionate toward her—Physical contact is essential for women. Many men find it difficult to show affection because of the way they were raised. Boys are expected to be strong as they grow up. They can't cry and they're not supposed to need anyone or anything. But the truth of the matter is that women are a different story. Affection speaks volumes to them.

The level of physical affection between a man and a woman speaks louder than words. Over the years, many couples become distant, sleep in separate beds, live respectfully under the same roof like brother and sister, but they are indifferent to each other. When he wants to be physically intimate, he wakes her up at night and says, "Come on, babe." He wants her to be in the mood, and yet day after day, week, or month he has not shown her one bit of affection.

Sometimes a husband is ashamed to kiss or hug his wife in public. Others don't even like to hold hands. Women have these needs, especially when they're stressed out. And when he denies her this physical contact, she feels rejected. If you want your wife to feel appreciated, loved, and crazy about you in bed, then know that this show of affection must always be present in your relationship, especially the times when you are not in bed.

Some women have no desire for physical affection because of past traumas and abuse. These cases should receive specialized help.

Cristiane:

I've always heard men say that women are complicated, we don't know what we want, that men have to stop being men in order to please us, but now you can understand where these myths came from. Okay, we're a bit complicated (okay, a lot), but that's because of our insecurities, which have already been explained. It's in our DNA. But this does not mean that we're hard to please. The problem is we are very different from men. What a man does not consider important is very important for a woman, and vice-versa. It's easy to say that women don't know what they want. The real question is: isn't this a good reason for men to stop criticizing and pay more attention to us?

As a woman, I've overcome much insecurity, but unfortunately, because of nature, I have to continue to fight it on a daily basis. This is a female battle that never ends. Just because you showed your wife some affection one day last week, that doesn't mean you've done your part. Love and appreciation have to be shown through a combination of things you do.

When women love, they give themselves completely. In fact, they love to give themselves to people. They're always thinking of every-one else first, even those who dislike them. As her husband, you have much to gain from this feminine trait she has, but be careful: when a woman gets tired of giving, it may be too late for you to change.

TASK

FOR HUSBANDS:

Which of your wife's basic needs do you need to pay more attention to? What are you going to do about this from now on, so that she feels appreciated and loved?

FOR WIVES:

How can you help your husband understand your basic needs, without being demanding or imposing?

 /BulletproofMarriage

On our Facebook page: fb.com/ BulletproofMarriage – **Men, post:** *Now I know how to make my wife feel valued and cared for. #Bulletproofmarriage*

 @BulletproofMate

Men, tweet: *Now I know how to make my wife feel valued and cared for. #BulletproofMarriage @BulletproofMate*

Women, post: *I am helping my husband understand what I need from him the most. #Bulletproofmarriage*

Women, tweet: *I am helping my husband understand what I need from him the most. #BulletproofMarriage @BulletproofMate*

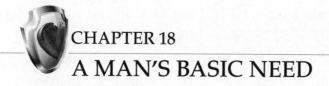

CHAPTER 18
A MAN'S BASIC NEED

Before we deal with the needs of men (a hint for women: it's not just sex), let's refer back to our friends from Eden, Adam and Eve. Earlier, we spoke about how God created them with shared authority over the earth. Nothing leads us to understand that he was more important than her, or that she was regarded as less than him. When God created Eve, His first thought was to make a partner, a helper who was suitable for Adam.[16] Together, they would be happier and more equipped than alone.

When God created woman, He gave her certain attributes that Adam did not have: femininity, gentleness, sensuality, motherhood, heightened emotions, sweetness, magnetism, thoroughness, organizational skills . . . to name a few. The combination of these unique female qualities made Eve naturally attractive to Adam. He wanted her by his side. When Adam saw Eve for the first time, he must have cried out: "That's worth a man leaving Mom and Dad for!"[17] Up to that moment, he'd not seen anything like her . . . There's no way he wanted to lose her. This is why every man has a natural desire to please a woman. When a man falls in love with a woman, he is bowled over by her. This

---

[16] Genesis 2:18, 20.
[17] Genesis 2:24.

can prove dangerous when a woman is unwise—not only for him, but for her too, since whatever happens to him will affect her. And that's exactly what happened.

Eve used her female charm and persuaded Adam to do what was wrong. Right away God realized that this power had to be controlled. If she was capable to influence him that way, and he was powerless to resist, then something had to be done to balance things out. In other words, God recognised that Eve was stronger than Adam. His obvious weakness, combined with her attractiveness, put her in a position of great power and influence over her husband. This is why part of the curse that fell on her was: . . . *and he shall rule over you.*

This is when the idea of man being the head and woman being the body came into being. In other words, she would need to (insert scary soundtrack here) submit to him. Women, wait! Before you slam this book shut and angrily throw it in the garbage basket, let me explain what this really means. Submitting to your husband most probably does not mean what you think. Let me take advantage of a woman's ability to add a special touch to things and allow my wife to disarm this time bomb . . .

THE POISONING OF A WORD

Cristiane:

Thanks a million, Honey!

Women, please read these words carefully because they were written to us:

Wives, understand and support your husbands in ways that show your support for Christ. The husband provides leadership to his wife the way Christ does to his church, not by domineering but by cherishing. So just as the church submits to Christ as he exercises such leadership, wives should likewise submit to their husbands. (Ephesians 5:22–24, MSG)

In the past, "submit" did not have the same negative connotation that it does today—thanks to the poison injected into this word by men and women who understand little about this concept. A concept that was positive and virtuous has now become a swear word for many women. When you ask a woman in today's society to submit to her husband, in her mind you might as well ask her to become a Neanderthal. If people think that submission to a husband means being a doormat, allowing him to be chauvinistic and hit her on the head with a club and drag her by the hair—then I agree, no woman should submit. But, submission in the original sense of the word, as designed by God, has nothing to do with that.

Submitting does not mean you lose your personality. Nor does it mean a chauvinistic control over women. It's simply a smart way of creating partnerships in marriage. The biblical sense of this word is really about encouraging humility, gentleness, understanding, confidence in another person's leadership, flexibility, kindness, and respect—the polar opposite of being defiant, rebellious, stubborn, and resistant. This means that a wife needs certain qualities to work in partnership with her husband, whom she should respect as a leader. Did you notice that the verse above says the wife "should" submit and let her husband lead? Notice how much power we possess! We are so strong that God feels He has to tell us that we should allow our husbands to lead us . . . Yes, allow. Otherwise, we end up taking charge . . . But He wants us to use our strength differently, in a wiser way.

First of all, we need to understand that being submissive does not mean we are inferior to our husbands. It's simply a role that you need to fulfil so that the partnership known as marriage will function properly. Wherever two or more people plan to work together for a common goal, someone has to lead and someone has to submit. Every country has a leader, every sports team has a coach, every company has a boss, and every school has a principal. In all these examples, the concepts of leadership and submission work together. This never means that the leader is a better person than the one who submits to leadership. They are simply fulfilling two different, complementary roles.

By the way, no matter what your circumstance might be as a woman in society, you already submit to various authorities and leaders—many of whom you do not know and probably do not even like. But you have to submit for the proper functioning of society or the group you belong to. This is the practical side of being submissive. It's essential to every group or society with common goals. Now, take a look at how strange this is: we're encouraged to submit to leaders we don't even know, while at the same time we rebel against the husbands who love us! Let's be smart about this. Submission is a smart way of dealing with the partnership known as marriage.

But you might ask, "Why do I have to submit to him, and not he to me?" Let's be honest ladies: would you feel a sense of accomplishment after taking the lead from your husband and forcing him to take a back seat in the marriage? You'd no longer have a man by your side. No woman likes a man who doesn't take the initiative, one who waits to be ordered around and given instructions all the time and is weak. The truth is women despise and are turned off by men like that.

Believe me when I say: we don't need to lead. We have another strength, which is the power of influence. With this, we can get whatever we want from our husbands. The power of influence is nothing more than submission carried out with wisdom. Remember, a husband is already "sold" on his wife. He wants to please her. The husband may be the head, but his wife is the neck. If she's wise, she can turn the head whichever way she wants . . . This is so scary that we have to be careful with this power so as not to destroy our husbands and ourselves.

One thing we heard the most in our Houston counseling sessions was this type of frustration: "My husband never takes the lead. I'm left to resolve everything at home. I can't take it anymore!" Little did they know that often it was their own fault . . .

When a woman does not submit to her husband, she ends up unintentionally castrating him. Though she doesn't mean to, she makes him out to be a nobody. Without respect, a man loses his masculinity. When you do not give him this role in the marriage, he does not feel respected and fails to fulfill his role as the man of the house.

A TRUE LEADER

The flip side of this subject is that when the Bible addresses the subject of a wife's submission, it already assumes a husband's biblical leadership. Women were not obliged to submit to leaders who mistreated them, but rather to leaders who sacrificed and gave themselves to them. A leader treats a woman as an extension of himself—a leader in the spirit of the Lord Jesus. A true leader wants the best for his followers. Therefore, when he leads, he tries to do what is best for those under his leadership. A wise husband who wants his wife to be submissive should lead in this fashion. He should gain the respect of his follower.

A true leader is not a dictator. He seeks out and listens to the opinions and needs of his followers. His decisions benefit everyone, not just himself. This is why his leadership engenders respect and does not need to be forced on others. A leader creates harmony in his relationships: he seeks the best for his team, and in turn, they believe in his leadership and gladly submit without resistance. This is how God designed it to be: man and woman, head and body in perfect harmony.

However, please note: women, to a much greater degree, hold the power to create this harmony in marriage. They are the ones who are invited to "allow" their husbands to lead them. The power is in her hands, and if she knows how to use this power, she will never lack a thing. What few people understand is that those who are genuinely submissive rarely have to submit. Because I am submissive to Renato, we rarely ever do things his way. A wife who submits to her husband can get whatever she wants from him. He is so grateful for the respect she gives him that he wants to please her, and so he ends up doing whatever she wants. Women, if your head's spinning because what you're reading sounds so different from anything you've ever heard— take a deep breath, stop, and reread this section. This is one of the simplest yet most ignored truths in the history of humanity!

However, make no mistake. Just as it's a sacrifice for men to show their feelings to their wives, it's also a sacrifice for women to let their husbands lead them. It goes against her nature, and this is where many end up losing in their love lives. They're obsessed about not "losing" in the relationship, when in fact the women who submit to their husbands actually win.

And before I close: husbands, if you're bad leaders, if you don't make your wives feel secure, if you're selfish when it comes to decisions and careless in your behavior (e.g., given over to addictions), if you neglect their needs or fail to use all your strength to care for them—how do you expect them to submit? That's why a wife's submission ceases to exist when her husband starts to act in a way that will hurt her. If he insists on being a bad leader and wants to walk straight off a cliff, she cannot be expected to follow him. She's going to let him walk off that cliff all by himself.

And so when a husband satisfies the basic needs of his wife—makes her feel appreciated, loved, and safe at his side—then submission will be a very natural thing for her . . . even though at times she may have to hold herself back and let him lead. Now we're ready to understand and explore the basic need of men: respect.

MEN WANT MEAT AND POTATOES

In my journey through the land of couples counseling, I've seen almost everything (I say "almost" because there's always someone who surprises us with a behavior we've never seen before). But when it comes to men, in particular, I've come to the conclusion that we are uncomplicated and easy to please. I have seen men put up with various things from their wives without complaint: a lack of intimacy, having to eat out every day because she doesn't want to cook, babysitting while she goes out with friends, going into debt after she spends all the savings, bouts of PMS, and enduring Celine Dion concerts. Some men are true heroes. But there's one thing that I have not seen: a man who puts up with the disrespect of his wife.

Take away everything from a man, but don't take away his respect. It's the meat and potatoes of his relationship. As I think about it, men don't ask for much. But many have not even received that from their wives. And you already know what happens when a basic need is not met. That person falls back on his basic animal instincts and comes out fighting in survival mode.

When a husband isn't given the respect he deserves inside his own home, he will look for it elsewhere . . . and there are two main ways for a man to fill this void: a fulfilling job or another woman.

Success at work satisfies a man's need for respect. People admire and appreciate him, he's in demand, and all this makes him feel valued. So what does he do? He dives deeper into his work in an attempt to get more respect. If a woman comes along, a common event in the lives of successful men, and appreciates him in ways that his wife does not, we arrive at the formula of "how to end a marriage."

Because of this, a wise wife will not argue or be reluctant to satisfy this basic need of her husband. She simply satisfies it. And this is how she does it. Take a look:

She talks up his strength—When a wife makes her husband feel strong, she's showing him respect. Unfortunately, many have swallowed the Hollywood agenda and helped destroy their husband's masculine image of himself. They criticize him for not being "sensitive," embarrass him in public, belittle him, and make no secret of it. There are women who make nasty comments and jokes about their husbands in the presence of others, and even embarrass them in front of their children. Many children no longer respect their fathers because their mothers don't. Unknowingly, many women have robbed their men of their strength.

He sees himself as weak and doesn't even attempt to initiate bold moves because his wife continually reminds him of his incompetence. These wives are shooting themselves in the foot. Once his confidence is destroyed, he'll turn into a failure. Words offend and sadden men to the point that they feel defeated and powerless. How can a man make his wife feel secure when all this is going on?

A wise woman makes her husband feel like a hero, as if he could conquer the world. She lifts him up in word and attitude and praises his strengths both inside and outside the home. In this way she prepares him for the world, and together they reap the benefits of his achievements.

She lets him be the head—She practices the concept of intelligent submission, which we explained earlier. During the few arguments they have, in which they can't reach an agreement, she lets him have the last word (of course, nothing that would be harmful to her). A wife should respect her husband's right to say "yes" or "no." Even when she knows, or thinks she knows, what his answer will be, she should consult him before doing anything. This way she reinforces the idea that his decision is valuable and important to her.

A common problem found in many of today's marriages is "the unimportant husband," who decides he's no longer going to play the marriage game. Since she doesn't respect anything he says, he stops offering his opinion and being a leader. Whether or not he agrees with an issue, she never listens. When she wants to do something, she doesn't care what he thinks. Because of this, he takes the following stance: "Go ahead. Do whatever you want. Clearly, what I think doesn't matter. Whether I agree or disagree, you're going to do it anyway, so go ahead." Hurt and reluctant, he relinquishes the decision-making to her. His wife may think she's gaining the upper hand, but in fact she's emasculated her husband. Ironically, these are the women who constantly complain about their husbands having no initiative and never participating in anything. Women, please understand: men don't want to be a part of something they know they're *always* going to lose. They will simply stop participating.

A wise woman can virtually get anything out of her husband. All she has to do is let him think it was his idea . . . Cristiane has become an expert at this! The secret is to bring the matter up to him, give him all the necessary information to make a decision, and then let him decide. If by chance his decision is not what you wanted, go along with it anyway. The seed has been planted. In the near future, his natural inclination to please a woman will drive him to do something for you about that matter.

She is his number-one fan—She admires her husband in spite of his faults. She's a true fan. One characteristic of a true fan is that she will keep rooting for her man even when he's losing. It's like your favorite sports team. They can lose ten games in a row, be the laughing stock of the sports world, and be in last place—but you still cheer them on in the hope that they'll win one day. This is what it means to be a fan.

Every man needs to feel admired because achievements are very important to him. But like every other man, he has flaws. A wise wife will not continuously criticize or point the finger at his flaws. Instead, she will search for things to admire about him. Her admiration works on his subconscious thoughts and eventually steers him to be the man she always wanted him to be. She praises his positive qualities and pretends not to notice the negative ones. There's nothing more demoralizing to a man than for his wife to be his main critic.

Acknowledge him in front of others—It's natural for women to talk about what's stressing them out, confiding in friends, mothers, or any other person. But here is the danger: you expose your husband's flaws to others. Why not be an ambassador for your husband? Build up his reputation and strengthen the respect you have for him.

Make yourself attractive to him—Being physically attracted to his wife is a basic need for a man. Men are much more visual than women; therefore, women should take care of their appearance. It puzzles me why many women are much more careful about this before marriage than after. They probably think they've now captured their man, so they no longer have to try so hard. But if he likes her with a little makeup, she should put it on out of love and keep the chemistry going between them. At times, because a husband knows how sensitive his wife can be, he doesn't ask her to do any of this. But she should be well aware of his needs. A wife should take care of herself to keep the flame alive. But, she should do this for her husband, not for other women, as very often happens. Find out what your husband likes. Some women want to be as thin as twigs because that's what society tells them to do, but their husbands may not like them so skinny. If magazines say that everyone's erasing their wrinkles (and facial expressions) with Botox, she blindly follows. But when her husband mentions how he'd love to see her in red lipstick, she quickly says she doesn't like that.

What is all important for women's magazines and their readers is not always important for a woman's husband. A classic example of this is cellulite. Women panic over a hint of cellulite, but most men don't even know what that is!

Cristiane:

As women, we should not try to compete with the photoshopped models in magazines. Instead, we should invest in our femininity, which is guaranteed to grab our husband's attention. Femininity is an important part of a woman's beauty, even though fashion has stopped paying attention to it.

Years ago, I used to complain about my nose because it wasn't a perfect, upturned nose like those I saw on magazine models. I even looked into getting it "fixed." But the thought came when it was already too late. I was married. Renato would not let me get it done, and over time, he taught me to like my nose. Then I realized that I had wanted to change my nose because of what society had been telling me, not because I needed to. Renato has always said my nose was one of my facial features that caught his eye the most!

Sometimes we want to make ourselves prettier for the wrong reasons and end up ignoring what really matters to our husbands. A few years ago I found out that what Renato finds most sexy about me is my self-confidence, which was not always high. This means that when I was trying to find myself and kept changing my hair, the style of my clothes, and my makeup, I was not sexy to him! My insecurities and attempts to change had not benefitted my marriage in any way.

A confident woman is an interesting catch for a man. After all, men are hunters. What if you were hunting in a forest, all decked out in camouflage, rifle at the ready, carefully moving closer to your prey . . . Suddenly, the deer notices you. But instead of running away, it trots up to you and says: "Shoot me with your rifle. Kill me. Take me home!" Without a doubt, you'd lose all interest! The intrigue of hunting comes down to the challenge of the chase.

In the same way, a woman's mystery is what captivates her husband. Her confidence motivates him to pursue her. Women, I said confidence—not making yourself unreachable or impossible to please.

She gives him space—Men need space, time to relax and deal with their stress. This is the "little nothing box" that we've already mentioned. Many wives don't even allow their husbands time to breathe. The poor guy hardly walks through the front door, and she's already piling all the stress of her day on top of him. A wise wife chooses the right time to talk, chooses what to say, and how to say it. This is so important for a man. He notices the respect and confidence she has, and appreciates the fact that she doesn't feel the need to keep bugging him about the same things all the time—she immediately becomes much more attractive to him.

Of course space has its limits. A husband who always wants space and never finds the time to talk to his wife is setting himself up for a slow death to his marriage. That will make her feel insecure and frustrated, and soon she won't be able to be the wife he needs and wants. Men, space is one thing, laziness is another. There is life outside the box!

BUT HE DOESN'T DESERVE IT

Remember, all we've explained so far in this chapter is about satisfying the basic needs of men, which is for a wife to give him respect. But you may be thinking that your husband doesn't deserve your respect because of all the negative things he does.

However, remember one thing: *the best thing you can do about a person's basic needs is meet them.*

The truth is that no one "deserves" anything. Women may say that their husbands don't deserve their respect, and men may say that their wives don't deserve their attention, but the fact of the matter is if you're still together and want a bulletproof marriage, you have to take care of each other. Don't just stand there waiting for him or her to deserve it. *Do what you have to do,* and in the end you'll see that your partner was worth all the effort.

Wives: Respect your husband because this is the only way to get anything out of him.

Husbands: Make your wife feel valued and cared for, and you'll reap the fruit of this effort all the days of your life.

WHEN HIS BASIC NEEDS ARE HERS AND VICE-VERSA

After one of our courses in Houston, where we explained the basic needs of men and women, a wife asked: "I think I'm the man in this relationship. What you said I need, and what he wants as well, and what I'm always asking him to give me is respect. What should I do?" She was a police woman. She was used to being tough and unemotional, and she had married a husband who liked . . . attention.

In recent times, this scenario has become more common. This is not difficult to understand with women's lib and the effeminate tendencies of some men in the last few decades. We've noticed that when a man is very emotional, his wife tends to compensate by being more rational because two emotional people aren't going to get very far. But it's only a matter of time before she starts to complain because even independent women like a strong man by their side.

This new phenomenon creates confusion for some couples. An emotional husband wants respect, but isn't doing what he should do to earn it, and a rational wife wants security, but finds she is unable to trust her husband . . .

If you find yourselves in a similar situation, here's what you should do:

- Emotional husbands, you have to overcome your insecurities in order to make your wife happy. Be less emotional and more rational. Be reassuring and mature around your wife.
- If you're an independent, rational, even bossy wife, you need to be more balanced. Allow your husband to make decisions in the relationship. Invite him to make decisions with you. Let him have the last word.

If each of you takes on the correct role, you'll be able to walk together for the rest of your life.

Cristiane:
I'm pickier about details when compared to Renato, and I tend to think about things that he forgets. On the other hand, he's much more rational than me, he gives things a lot more thought than I do, and he is less impulsive. He's strong. When we're in difficult situations and I want to cry and hide in a corner, he comes with his strength, hugs me, and makes me feel protected.

A wise wife recognizes her husband's attributes and vice-versa.

I would never have imagined the chapter on men's basic needs would turn out to be longer than the women's chapter . . . Why is that? It is because of your strength, woman. It takes more words to convince you . . . Use this strength wisely.

 TASK

FOR WIVES:

Which of your husband's basic needs do you need to be more dedicated to satisfying? What are you going to do from now on to make sure he feels respected?

FOR HUSBANDS:

How can you help your wife understand your needs without being demanding or imposing?

 /BulletproofMarriage

Men, post: *I'm helping my wife understand what I need from her the most. #Bulletproofmarriage*

 @BulletproofMate

Men, tweet: *I'm helping my wife understand what I need from her the most.*

 On our Facebook page fb.com/ BulletproofMarriage— **Women, post:** *Now I understand my husband and what he really needs. #Bulletproofmarriage*

 Women, tweet: *Now I understand my husband and what he really needs. @ BulletproofMate #BulletproofMarriage*

CHAPTER 19
SEX

First of all, I want to welcome all the men who want to bullet-proof their marriages. This is probably the first chapter you are actually interested in reading. And to the sexually frustrated women: a light has just appeared at the end of the tunnel. There's a reason why this chapter is almost at the end of this book. Putting everything you learned in the previous chapters into practice is what will contribute to a great sex life. If you have ignored everything that was said up till now, then you probably will only glean a small amount of help from this chapter. So if you've skipped over chapters to get to this one more quickly, go back and read them over first. I guarantee it'll be well worth it!

A healthy sex life is one of the main tools in a bulletproof marriage. It never hurts to remind people of this. The quickest way to assess the health of a relationship is to find out how they're doing in bed. If my wife and I could ask a couple only one question during a counseling session to find out how they're doing, it would be: "How's your sex life?"

Sex in a marriage is like glue that holds the couple together. It's the mystery that makes two into one, literally and also in all other respects. Sex says a lot. It expresses feelings and thoughts that words cannot express. When you don't seek to be physically intimate with your partner, your attitude tells them things in their head, such as, "I'm not good enough for him/her. Why is he/she ignoring me? Does he/she have someone else? There must be something wrong with how I look. He/she must not want me around anymore." On the other hand, when a couple has a healthy and active sex life, the unspoken messages are: "My husband finds me attractive. My wife is happy with me. We satisfy each other. There's no reason for my husband/wife to look at anyone else." The consequences of these mental messages can build up or destroy a marriage. Ignore this at your own risk.

Not only does sex speak, it heals many problems in a relationship. It is scientifically proven that intimacy has a cleansing effect—it is a mental and physical detox for the couple. And so we can safely conclude, the less you do it, the more distant you will feel, and the more problems you will experience. In a sexless marriage, any small problem will be multiplied by a thousand. On the other hand, it's rare for a couple to have a bad morning after a great night in bed . . . Little things are brushed off because both have good credit emotionally—where sex is the strongest currency.

You can easily guess whether or not a couple is doing well sexually by observing their moods. Irritation, indifference, and lack of caring are sure signs that a couple's bed is only being used for sleep. This is how powerful sex is.

The message is: be intimate, do it well, and do it regularly. But for many couples this is easier said than done. Let's unravel this mystery.

WHERE IT BEGINS AND ENDS

Counter to what many may think, sex is not what happens when a husband and wife undress and sleep together. To better understand this, think of a sandwich. When you want a sandwich, the first thing you think of is what kind you want . . . chicken, beef, turkey, etc. But that's not all that goes into a sandwich. You also decide on the type of bread, whether you want cheese, onion, lettuce, tomato, mustard, pickle . . . all those things that complement and enhance the flavor of the meat in your sandwich. You could just eat the meat by itself, but everything else makes it taste so much better.

The same goes for sex. Clearly, it is two bodies engaged in a physical act, but the act itself is simply the protein in the sandwich. It comes in the middle, but what happens before and after that act are the true beginning and end of what we call great sex. The before and after involve the mind. Yes, sex begins and ends in the mind. The physical act is the vehicle of expression, but the mind is the driver and the destination, all at the same time. Women usually do this better than men. For them, sex is connected to everything else. Remember the wires in the female brain? She can be aroused by things that would never arouse a man, simply because she associates everything with everything else.

And so, husbands, don't be surprised when you take the initiative at home and take out the rubbish, for example, only to have your wife looking at you as if she wants to take you straight into the bedroom when you come back in. Don't try to understand, just enjoy it!

For men, on the other hand, sex is very straightforward. All he needs to get in the mood is for her to be present. It's as if men simply have an on and off button when it comes to sex. Women, on the other hand, are like the cockpit of the new Boeing 787, with buttons all over the place, and men don't know where to start. If he presses the wrong button, fasten your seat belt and put on your oxygen mask!

So here is a special hint for men:

Sex starts above the neck.

Men often come and ask us for advice and say something such as: "My wife's never in the mood . . . She always has an excuse . . . It's like I enjoy sex and she doesn't . . . I don't want her to feel as if she's doing me a favor . . . Once a month seems great for her, and sometimes that's even too much . . ."

Listen: sex is very, very different for women compared to men. The mistake many husbands make is to assume that women look at sex the way they do—the physical pleasure of relieving tension. Let's use another food analogy (we're all going to get hungry in a little bit). Women see sex as the cherry on top of the intimacy cake. It's an expression of the intimacy, friendship, and love between the two of you—not just in bed, but throughout the day.

Have you ever just eaten the fruit without the cake? It can be a bit tart and lacking in taste all by itself, right? It doesn't satisfy your hunger, and you need something to balance out its taste. Well, this is how women see sex that's not preceded by intimacy. Tart but meaningless. It won't be something she looks forward to doing again. But when the cherry is on top of a cake, it's a whole other story. The cake offers substance, and the cherry enhances the flavor—a great combination.

The cake is the intimacy that precedes the bedroom. When a woman hears the word *intimacy*, what comes to mind is a *deep conversation*, while men will think about putting their hands certain places. She is thinking that she is going to really learn what her husband is thinking about, especially if it's about her. She loves his attention being focused on her and what she says. This is what strengthens a couple's intimacy.

If you've only been giving your wife cherries, now you can understand her reaction. Be a better lover to your wife by becoming a better listener and conversationalist. Dedicate more time to the cake. Connect with her.

I'm not asking you to be a conniver, flattering her to get what you want. Rest assured that it won't take her long to notice your insincerity, and then you won't get even a cherry . . . I'm talking about having a sincere interest in the person who is inside your wife's body.

If you grasp the concept that for women sex begins above the neck, both of you will be much happier in bed and everywhere else, and there won't be enough cake for all the cherries . . .

I DON'T LIKE SEX

This is almost as ridiculous as saying, "I don't like air." The only difference is that nobody dies from a lack of sex. But saying you don't like sex is not reasonable unless there is something physically wrong with you. Sex is a *healthy thing and extremely pleasurable*. God created it . . . and God doesn't make bad things. If people say they don't like sex, it is because they don't know what it is, or they know but their partners don't. So if a husband likes sex and his wife doesn't, it's his responsibility to help her find out how good it can be for her. I say "for her" because the goal of intimacy is to satisfy your partner. Many women don't care to have sex because they feel their husbands use them for their own personal pleasure.

I want to make something very clear here: it's a husband's obligation to make sure his wife has an orgasm. The goal of sex is to please your partner, not to please yourself. Because of selfish attitudes like this, many end up saying, "I don't like sex." Everyone enjoys sex when it's done the way God intended—to completely satisfy your partner.

But for this to happen, both have to regard each other's pleasure as their top priority. The obvious, logical way of doing this would be to put a woman's pleasure first, then a man's. Women usually take longer than men, so if men think of themselves first, women will be left out in the cold.

To sum things up, sex is both a necessity and a pleasure, and it's an activity that strengthens and protects a marriage. What are some tips for a great sex life? We have five for you.

FIVE INGREDIENTS FOR A GREAT SEX LIFE

1. Clear your mind—First, clear your mind of any and all dirty thoughts about sex. You may have to purify your mind from all the warped information that you've accumulated from friends, magazines, pornography, and other questionable sources. There's an abundance of filth, distortion, and misinformation circulating out there about this subject. Understand one thing: when God created man and woman, they didn't need pornography or a manual to have sex. He designed sex for a couple's pleasure and enabled them to satisfy each other without the intervention of others. You and your partner are all you need to achieve great intimacy. So don't view sex as dirty or taboo. It is God's gift to you. It is one of the few things in life that is exclusive to both of you. Friendship is not exclusive to marriage. Neither is being faithful (you can be faithful to your job). But sex is exclusive to a couple. So treat it with the importance, purity, and value it deserves.

2. Use your mind to connect—Remember, sex is connected to everything that precedes the actual act, especially for women. Sex begins and ends in the mind. Take time with your mind to focus on the qualities you admire in your spouse. This is a conscious, voluntary decision you have to make, or else other concerns that have nothing to do with your partner will occupy your thoughts. Stress is the biggest factor for low sexual drive and impotence. You need to set aside time to mentally connect with your partner, no matter how busy or stressed you might be at your job or with other issues. Turn yourself off to whatever might try to divert your attention away from your spouse. Comment about her clothes, her beauty, his handsomeness, the parts of each other's bodies that you like the most; ask her what she's thinking about, her plans and projects, her concerns—listen carefully and offer help, encouragement, and security. Women should not expect men to be as open about their thoughts as girls are because men do not need to do this to feel "connected." But women should sprinkle their day with kind remarks, unexpected physical contact, a sexy look, a compliment about one of his manly traits—such as how strong he is, his determination, and his intelligence for business. All these things are pre-sex.

3. Focus on your partner—The pleasure you get from satisfying your partner should be as great as your own pleasure. In fact, this is one of the main secrets to making your husband or wife crazy about you. Your focus should be on your partner, not on yourself! If she reaches climax, yours will be the result of that. Think about what is important to the other person. A crucial point that normally differs between men and women is privacy. He might not consider it much of a problem if someone in the next room hears moans and groans. It adds to his manhood. On the other hand, if she doesn't have a heart attack first, she'll never be able to look that other person in the eye. Let's not even mention one of your children wandering into the room wanting to know what all the noise is about. So, men, focus on what's important to her. Women need to feel safe and private before they can loosen up. Lock the bedroom door. Soundproof your bedroom walls if necessary. Respect her and be discreet. In fact, women need to feel secure, not only when it comes to privacy but with your behavior as well. If you lie to her, hide information, are irresponsible with money, and have an unpredictable temper, she will not feel comfortable or safe with you. Didn't we warn you that women connect sex to everything else? Now here's a tip for the women: if your husband tries really hard to make you reach the clouds, then right after, make him reach the stars. It's your turn to focus on him . . .

4. Discover and explore each other—Nobody is the same. What one woman thinks is amazing, another woman may hate. This is why you should be each other's lovers and find out what excites your partner.

What parts of her body does she like you to touch? What does she not like to be touched? Ask your wife, explore her likes and dislikes rather than consult websites and magazines for this information. These things are very personal. Some men like (or have read that women like) something that causes their wives to feel uncomfortable during sex. You commonly find things like "seven ways to drive your man crazy in bed" on magazine covers. Things like this sell because people are very ignorant about the subject, and so they fill their minds with this junk. Be extremely careful with what you bring into your mind and bedroom. Not everything that's in magazines (actually, almost nothing) is good for you. Sexual pleasure comes from exploring the person you're married to. I don't care if a magazine says that women like this or that. What if my wife doesn't like it? Not all women are the same. They aren't robots, nor were they all created as carbon copies of each other. Couples need to dialogue, converse with each other, find out what each other enjoys, and adapt to each other. It is also important to find out how frequently your spouse would like to be intimate. For example, having sex once a week might be enough for her. On the other hand, her husband wants to have sex every day. In this case, they need to agree on a middle ground. She'll have to be a bit more understanding and agree to be sexually intimate at least three times a week, and he'll have to sacrifice and be happy with only three times a week . . . or twice . . . or four times. What is important is that you adapt to each other. Never impose something on your spouse, especially sex. When it's forced and not natural, it will be very unpleasant. When something is not good for one partner, it's not good for either person. Respect each other's boundaries. For example, if you like oral sex and your partner doesn't, don't force the situation.

5. Invest in foreplay—When was the last time you gave each other a passionate kiss . . . or gave your partner a lengthy massage? Have you caressed your wife lately? Have you run your fingers through her hair, touched her neck, and ended with a hug? The romance that unfolds during the day and the hours before intimacy come to a climax when both actually engage in the act. This moment requires a great deal of self-control from men. Studies show that on average men ejaculate two to three minutes after penetration. On the other hand, women need an average of seven to twelve minutes to reach orgasm. Can you see where the problem lies? Men need to climb the mountain slowly so as not to reach the top just as their wives are putting on their boots . . . This is when a smart man, who's been practicing all the steps we've explained so far in this book, has an advantage. A woman who's been romanced over the last twenty-four hours will not need as much warming up before the actual act. However, men still need to control themselves and keep at their wives' pace instead of rushing ahead. Women can help their husbands by maintaining a more active sex life. If he has sex with you once a month or less, it'll be difficult for him to control himself when you're together.

WAIT, IT'S NOT OVER YET!

We said that sex begins and ends in the mind, and the actual act in itself is just the filling of the sandwich. This means that after both have reached orgasm (yes, this is the goal), intimacy itself is still not over. Of course, at this point, both are physically satisfied, and a man in particular might feel like rolling over and going to sleep—but not men who've read *Bulletproof Marriage*! They know that the moments immediately after sex are when their wives are feeling closer and more connected with them than ever. And so, this is when he needs to maintain the physical contact, show affection, say sweet things, and pay compliments. You cannot under any circumstances allow your wife to feel used. Understand that this is the best time to make her feel loved and—honestly—to begin to prepare her for the next time!

THE MOTHER-IN-LAW I ASKED GOD FOR

Cristiane:

Shortly before I got married, when I was still very young and inexperienced, my mother taught me something about sex that I've always kept in mind: "You won't always feel like making love with your husband, but don't go by what you feel. Do it anyway. Once you start, you'll end up enjoying it. Never say 'no' to him, so that he never feels rejected."

Up to this very day, Renato thanks her for this advice!

Both men and women like sex. I don't believe the myth that says women like it less than men. The problem is many men don't know how women view it. For her, sex is the climax of a day filled with love: dialogue, caresses, caring, glances, patience, and everything else that is good and triggered by the love her husband has shown her throughout the day. When a husband puts this into practice, his wife will probably end up wanting to have sex more often than he . . .

However, the truth is you won't be showered with romance every single day. There will be bad days and normal days. Don't expect every night or every intimate moment to be marked by fire and passion. That just doesn't happen. Don't live in the fantasy world of movies. There are times when you'll have to begin the act when you're not really in the mood. At times your partner will want to be intimate, and you won't feel like it. But when this happens, just decide to get in the mood. Don't be lazy. Go ahead, participate. Never reject your partner. Remember, sex talks. One unreasonable rejection can create little monsters inside your spouse's head. This is why couples should make love even when they're tired. With the busy lifestyles we have today, who isn't tired at the end of the day? One thing is certain: the more you do it, the more you'll want to do it; the less you do it, the less you'll want to do it.

This is such a serious matter that the Bible itself says[18] you don't have the right to deny your husband or wife when they want to be sexually intimate. Women are not meant to be their husband's sex slave. The explanation given in the Bible is much more beautiful and profound: your body is not yours, it's his, and his body is not his, it's yours. You belong to each other. If one denies pleasure to the other, he will be breaking the covenant of marriage, and giving room for the devil to act. (There are many people who are opening the doors of their marriage to the devil because of this.)

When one of you is sexually frustrated because the other is always unavailable, adultery often occurs—a major cause of broken marriages. Obviously, if the reason you are holding back has to do with pain or some other physical difficulty, you need to speak to each other and seek medical help.

PHASES AND STAGES

A warning sign along the road of a couple's sexuality: stay tuned to the phases and stages of your marriage and life. Certain events, factors, and changes will inevitably affect your intimacy. This doesn't necessarily mean things will get worse, but you have to adapt and be more understanding of each other. Something you will have to bear in mind is that sex at fifty is not the same as in your twenties. Another thing to bear in mind is any large difference in age—for example, he is forty-five and she is thirty-five.

Immediately after a pregnancy, women tend to be less interested in sex. Husbands need to understand that the arrival of a child changes everything in a marriage. His wife will be tired from taking care of the baby (if you don't think so, try taking care of a baby for twenty-four hours and see for yourself), her body will have changed, and

---

[18] 1 Corinthians 7:3–5.

she will be sleep deprived. Husbands have to understand and reduce their expectations in this department. His wife, however, should not use this as an excuse. Her sexual desire may have decreased, but his is still the same . . . The baby needs you, but also a father. Do not neglect your husband.

When a man is going through tough times at work, his sexual drive also tends to decrease. Failure at work may be demoralizing to a man and can even cause impotence. Wives should wisely support their husbands and make them feel "manly" by constantly admiring, supporting, and encouraging them.

Different work schedules (that keep the couple apart), long trips, and health issues are other factors that can affect a couple's sexual activity. My advice is that you remain alert to these signs and make the necessary changes so that they do not affect you negatively.

CAN WE DO THAT?

Few subjects raise more doubt and questions than sex. We're constantly asked if this or that can be done during sex. Instead of answering all these questions in detail, I want to point out something important for all couples as a general guide.

The most sexually frustrated couples worry the most about this subject. They are usually women who are overly worried about the sexy lingerie they're going to wear (for most men, any kind of lingerie is sexy), visit sex shops, worry about what this or that magazine says about sex, are extremely concerned about weight gain and wondering what their husband is going to think. Or they could be men who've developed an addiction to pornography and masturbation, and who've stopped being their wives' real life lovers to fantasize about women they will never meet.

Remember: don't base your life on people who are not a good example of marital happiness. Celebrities and "relationship experts" who are glamorized by the media are for the most part unhappy in love. Married for the third or fourth time, divorced, cheating and being cheated on, or never able to find true love. If there is anyone who you should *not* want to receive love life advice from, it would be those people. And so, don't let the confusion of this world complicate what God made simple. Follow these common-sense rules: be your husband's or wife's lover. Explore and discover each other. Don't impose or demand that your partner do anything they do not want to do. Do not do anything that goes against nature (anal sex). Focus on pleasing your partner and do not be selfish. The rest, you will develop on your own.

If you want to check out our answers on several other specific questions about sex, visit our website at www.bulletproofmarriage.org/sex.

TASK:

Need I spell it out what you should do now?

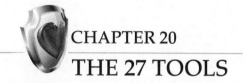

CHAPTER 20
THE 27 TOOLS

Over the course of our marriage and after years of counseling couples with a wide variety of marital problems, Cristiane and I have developed what we call "tools" to deal with all sorts of situations that might arise. Some of these we created for ourselves, and others we learned or acquired from other wise couples. We've selected the best and outlined them in this chapter for you to have at your disposal.

Every household should have a toolbox. You need one when you want to hang pictures, fix a wobbly drawer, or unclog a drain. Every marriage needs specific tools as well. The twenty-seven listed here will help you repair and maintain your marriage. Most likely they won't all apply to the situations you're in right now, but this information will help you assemble your own toolbox to use in marriage emergencies. Like any other toolbox, you don't need all of the items to do one job, but it's always good to have them handy, because you never know when they might be needed.

Most of these are tools that you probably already know, but aren't putting into practice. Their strength lies in using them in tandem with other tools, which may be why you haven't seen results when you only used one tool on its own. So rally your strength and apply them again, but this time combine them as needed. You may not have had any results before reading this book because you didn't know then what you do now. Open up your toolbox and start adding the following tools inside, one by one—and learn how to apply them in the right situations.

1. Don't sleep on it

Don't go to bed with an unresolved issue between you. Believing that you can resolve them later will only make the problems worse. The Scriptures say, *"Be angry and do not sin: do not let the sun go down on your wrath, . . . nor give place to the devil."*[19] In other words, it's not a sin to be angry, but it is a sin to let your anger linger into the following day, often causing you to do something irrational because of it. They say that time heals all wounds, but this is hardly ever true. An open wound only gets worse with time. Problems start off like brand-new baby green monsters—fragile, small, and seemingly harmless. They feed off of silence and indifference, and grow while you sleep. If no one does anything about them, you end up with giant green monsters as pets that chew up your marriage and tear you both apart. The sooner you kill them (preferably, while they're still unhatched), the less the damage they cause. It's easy to know whether or not you've killed your monster. If you're sleeping with your backs to each other or in separate rooms, it means that the issue hasn't been resolved yet, and the monster is still terrorizing your marriage. Talk it over again and reconcile with your partner. This tool was something that Cristiane and I developed to solve our problem of the silent treatment. We agreed: "From now on, whenever we have a problem, let's stay up and talk about it until it's resolved." Of course this resulted in many nights of going to bed at three in the morning, but eventually we'd fall asleep in each other's arms. We'd

---

[19] Ephesians 4:26, 27.

wake up happy the next day, because we wouldn't drag any nega-
tivity from the previous day into the new day. When we were strict
about using this tool, the silent treatments ended. I learned how to
solve a problem once and for all. A problem stuck on the back burner
is a problem that only worsens. Many couples go through this. Your
spouse wants to resolve an issue, but you don't because you think
it's already been resolved, or because you're upset and don't want
to deal with it. Ignore your emotions and do what's right. Using the
"Ten Steps to Problem Solving," explained in chapter 6, will help
you with this. The words *"nor give place to the devil"* in the verse
above reveal a lot. When you have unresolved issues that make you
angry, you are giving place to the devil. During any particular time
in your relationship, you're either in the presence of God or in the
presence of the devil. Please understand this. You should develop a
sensitivity to distinguish when you're in the presence of one or the
other. Watch for the signs, they're easy to see. When God is present,
your relationship goes well. When the devil is present, things are a
tangled mess. This means that he found a gap to squeeze into your
relationship. So hurry up and close that gap, now!

> *When to use this tool: if something is unresolved or left "up in the air";
> when you're holding something against your partner; when one is giv-
> ing the other the cold shoulder.*

2. Love never hurts

There's no excuse for hurting your partner physically, verbally,
emotionally, or any other way. Being angry is not an excuse for hurting
the other person. How many times do we get angry about something
that happens at work? So what do we do when that happens? Beat
up our boss? Kick the chairs? No, we learn how to manage our anger
without hurting others around us. You know that if you attack your

boss (or anyone else in the company), you'll lose your job, so you learn how to manage your anger to avoid any inappropriate behavior with co-workers. Do the same with your loved one. Never be aggressive toward them. And don't use the excuse that you're a nervous or short-tempered person. True love does not inflict pain. This also goes for hurtful words that can erupt when a couple is having an argument. They swear at each other as though their spouse meant nothing to them, but someone who is part of our own body should never be treated this way. Don't drag yourself into the gutter by swearing at your spouse or attacking their character.

Happy couples treat each other with higher standards. They refuse to accept harmful behavior. The lower the tolerance for bad behavior, the happier the couple will be over time. For example, when a wife swears at her husband and he retaliates, both break the rules of behaving in a civilized manner. If you don't fix the situation by apologizing and promising to never act like that again, forget it! Once you cross that line, you'll cross it again, until you end up reaching a point of no return. We counsel many couples who tell us about a recent argument and then say to each other: "Sorry, but I was just being honest and saying how I feel." You don't always need to say exactly what you feel. Our emotions can make us come up with crazy thoughts. Sometimes, how you feel isn't really what you think. If you act on impulse and blurt out your feelings, you inflict wounds that your spouse may not be able to recover from.

When to use this tool: when your emotions are about to get the better of you and you feel like you're about to explode. Memorize this phrase: "Love never hurts." Be civil. If your partner hurts your feelings, respectfully insist, without adding fuel to the fire, to treat each other with higher standards. You may have to talk about it later after tempers have calmed down, but don't let it get the better of you.

3. Do not generalize

However you complete these sentences, "You always . . ." and "You never . . ." Both will only cause problems. Don't use the brush of one situation to paint the entire character of your partner. "You *always* do what you like, *never* what I like." "You *never* listen to me." These types of statements are rarely ever true, and they will only anger your partner. Deal with the matter at hand and resist the temptation to connect it to the past. Watch out for the words *never, always, nothing, everything* and *every time.* These are absolute terms and leave no other options. Avoid them. This problem is most common in women. A wife *feels* like her husband always has *that attitude,* based on so many past experiences. She expresses what she is *feeling* and not just the facts. The problem is that if a woman says, "You never take me out," her husband will automatically remember that he took her out once two months ago. So he says, "I never . . . ? But I took you out to see that movie . . ." and flips the problem back onto her. When you generalize, your spouse won't deal with the problem you've just brought up, and will tend to remember a fact to disprove your statement. How do you deal with a problem if you constantly hear generalisations? Understand that she is probably not saying that you literally "never" or "always" do something. What she is expressing is how she feels about that situation. What she is really saying is: "This happens so often that I feel like you never take me out," instead of, "You never take me out." Be patient. Don't get irritated and keep the focus on the issue that she is bringing to the table and her need for you to help resolve it.

When to use this tool: Whenever you have a conversation. If generalizations are used at any point during the conversation, apologize and rephrase your words. If your partner constantly generalizes, pinpoint the problem, so that you don't repeat these inaccurate words in the future. Focus on what he or she is really saying and deal with it.

4. Stop nagging and start praying

Your partner repeatedly insists on doing things that irritate you, doesn't want to change, and you have been nagging for years, but nothing changes. Have you learned that it doesn't do any good to nag your spouse? Then nag God. Ask Him to touch your partner's heart and give you the wisdom to deal with your situation. Of course when someone feels attacked, they're focused on defending themselves. But God can make them see their own error. Prayer has a thousand and one uses. Besides being a tool that can bring about the changes that you can't create alone, it also helps you deal with stress as you place your anxieties in God's hands. He can handle all your frustration and anger with a problem over and over again for as long as it remains. You, on the other hand, wouldn't be able to withstand all of that. Think about it. You're turning to the One who created marriage to solve your problem. It's like complaining directly to the manufacturer, like calling customer service and speaking directly to the owner. But be persistent. Answers don't always appear overnight. Keep praying. Pray for yourself as well, so that you won't be part of the problem. Ask for wisdom to deal with the situation.

Cristiane:

When I realized that my constant nagging wasn't changing my husband, I came to the conclusion that I couldn't fix that situation alone and sought help from God. This tool is a change of direction: stop acting on emotion, and instead act on faith by trusting in God. But make no mistake, God is not a magician and He doesn't work alone. He does His part when you do your part. And if you don't know how to do your part, ask Him for guidance. Women tend to nag to the point of aggravation. We think that we can solve problems by complaining. I began praying and asking Him to change my own behavior. I wanted to stop crying about the problem and start acting by faith, and I was only able to do that through prayer. Only God can change your spouse. Only He can change someone from the inside out. Before, I prayed that God would change Renato, but after seeking God's guidance to show me what to do, I began to seek out ways to change myself first. And that was when I began noticing a change in my husband. God not only gives us comfort and peace, but He also guides us in what to do. This principle can work in every area of our lives.

When to use this tool: when all else fails.

5. Show appreciation

Married people will sometimes be drawn into an affair simply because they discover someone else who appreciates them more than their wife or husband. When you sense your partner is distant, or you yourself feel distant, you need to consciously make the effort to show your appreciation for your spouse. For example, cook him something he likes, make a special dinner, wash up and throw on some perfume as you wait for him, and be home when he comes home. Check in on her, call her during the day, notice her new outfit, go out with her and do something that she likes. It's very easy to take each other for granted after a few years of marriage. Various situations can divert a couple's focus, causing them to forget about each other over the years and slip into a phase of indifference. Once kids come along, they can consume all of a couple's energy. A woman's life can easily revolve around them, and her husband gets pushed aside. If both are struggling to grow a business or to pay off debts, their needs for appreciation get side-lined. Or when the children finally leave home and get married, a couple can feel as if they've become strangers, unable to relate to each other because they've lost that bond. The appreciation tool becomes very useful at these times. Identifying the phase of indifference is easy. Just take a look at the two. They are no longer a unit. Each one lives in his or her own little world. One in front of the TV, the other glued to the computer. One goes to sleep before the other. They go out alone, live separate lives and have very little in common. A couple who lives like this rarely shows each other any appreciation, because you need to notice others to appreciate them. But this can change, even after years of indifference, if you want it to. Remember the little things you did for each other while you were dating and early on in your marriage? Remember the care you had for each other? That's what needs to be brought back to the relationship. I'm going to repeat a sentence that you will often find throughout this book (something you can't forget): a happy marriage takes work. Even to this day I invest in my marriage. It's a constant but rewarding job.

A question I'd like every couple to memorize is: *what does my spouse need from me right now?* If you don't know, try to find out. (They won't always tell you. Or they might say "nothing," when the truth is, they have a long list of things listed in alphabetical order.) Ask yourself: "What can I do for him/her?" *She* may be feeling stressed or upset, in need of your company or encouragement. She turns to you because she knows that she has a strong person by her side. Sometimes just one word is enough, or even simply comforting her in silence, assuring her that everything will work out, that she's just going through a phase and together you will overcome it. If she's sick, she needs to feel cared for, or at least know that you care about what she's going through, even if someone else is caring for her.

Women, don't think that this job is only for men. Sometimes a man might be feeling dejected and needs to hear some encouraging words to show him that you still see him as strong. Warning: most men do not know how to receive compliments, but it doesn't mean they don't like them. You may have already tried to encourage him and seen no real response. A wife may compliment his clothes and he simply shrugs. Don't be discouraged! Believe me, he simply doesn't want to give away his feelings . . . This is quite common and involuntary, almost like a manufacturer's defect. Even if he does not know how to receive a compliment, don't stop complimenting him. You may not see his inner feelings, but don't worry, it really is working.

Psychologist John Gottman, a respected relationship expert, conducted a study that led him to conclude the following: for every negative experience a couple has, five positive experiences are required to compensate for the negative one. Let's say that a couple exchanged harsh words and hurt each other. If they want to make amends, they need to perform five positive actions in order to nullify that one negative experience. Gottman's theory leads us to believe that bad experiences are five times more powerful than good ones. For this reason, when a husband does something that makes his wife stop trusting him, she still clearly remembers what happened one month later. So the more you appreciate your partner, the more positive impressions you will accumulate in your relationship.

When to use this tool: always, especially when you start noticing a distance or indifference between you and your partner.

6. When your partner asks you to do something, do it first

Much of the stress in a relationship comes from the thought that we are not as important to our spouse as something or someone else. So when your partner asks you for something, put it at the top of your list. Make it a priority, so they don't need to ask you again. It's a simple rule of thumb, but it's worth its weight in gold.

A husband asks, "Honey, could you please buy me some razors when you go to the store. Mine is dull?" His wife answers with a, "Yeah, okay," but wasn't really paying much attention. The next day, he looks for the razors and they're not there. He gets a little upset but doesn't say anything. She apologizes and promises to buy more the next time. But then the story repeats itself the next day. Is it trivial? Yes, but couples fight over trivial things. Why do they fight? Because that triviality is actually whispering something very serious in their spouse's ear like: "I don't mean anything to you," "If your mother asked you to do something, you'd drop everything, run off and do it, but when I ask, you ignore me." That's the real problem. The razors aren't the problem. The problem lies in the hidden message behind your attitude. You should incorporate this rule into your daily life. When he or she asks you for something, get it done quickly, because this will solidify the fact that you come first in each other's lives. Think about it. When your boss asks you for something, you make a habit of getting it done as soon as possible. You know that person is important because they can influence what happens to you. Well then, how much truer is this in your marriage! Your husband/wife is far more important. Maybe your spouse has been asking you for something for quite a while and you haven't done it. It could be anything from something that seems trivial to a serious conversation that's been long overdue. Make it a priority and get it done right now, as evidence of your consideration.

When to use this tool: whenever he/she asks you for something.

7. Look after your looks

Many people who used to be really careful about their looks while they were dating see marriage as a "license to look ugly." If anything, it's after marriage that you need to look after yourself the most. Never take your partner for granted, assuming that you have already won him or her over. Purposefully seek to look beautiful for your partner. Watch your weight, how you dress, wear makeup (if your husband likes it). Cleanliness and tidiness of your home are very important too.

Some women don't like wearing makeup, but their husbands might enjoy seeing them in lipstick or eye shadow. A woman may think that her husband has to like her for her natural beauty: *This is the way I am.* Of course, I'm not going to like Cristiane just because of her earrings or makeup, but if a woman knows that her husband likes these things, she should make the effort to please him. The same goes for when it comes to food. If there is something you don't like, but he does, prepare that food for him just to please him.

That's what marriage is all about, living to please the other person, to make the other person happy. Okay, I agree that it's not fair to demand that a spouse become someone they aren't, but it won't kill you to make the effort to please your spouse, which isn't too much to ask, and in the end you'll feel better about yourself. At work, I have to wear a suit, tie, dress pants, dress shirt, and dress shoes. In my leisure time, I like flip-flops, shorts and T-shirts, because I almost never get to wear them. When we first got married, going to the movies meant that I would wear sweats and flip-flops, because I wanted to be comfortable. For her, this was a special date, so she'd get all dressed up. Just picture us together! She wouldn't say anything, but she felt embarrassed by me. When she finally said: "Those clothes make you look like you gave up on life," I got upset, but later I understood why. We rarely went out, so when we did, I had to honor her and dress accordingly. I make an effort because I love her, and because she likes it. But for me, I'd rather just go out in flip-flops!

We counseled a couple in which the husband was sexually frustrated. He complained that whenever he sought to be intimate with his wife, she rejected him. As he spoke, we noticed that she was embarrassed. We asked to speak to them separately, so they'd feel freer to speak in private. That's when she finally opened up: "He says I never want him to touch me, but couldn't he at least take a shower every day?" She had to be superwoman to endure intimate moments with a guy who had no clue about cleaning up after work. He was so used to a lack of hygiene that he didn't even realize it was driving a wedge between them. Something that was so easy to resolve! Soap, hot water, a towel and *voilà*! The end of their problems.

Cristiane:

You represent your spouse, so after you get married your responsibility about your looks is even more important. Your appearance says a lot about how you feel. When you're happy and feel accomplished, it reflects outwardly. If you love, respect, and value your husband, it's only natural that it shows. You could very well be unhappy on the inside and yet look good on the outside, but there is no way that you can be happy on the inside and look bad outwardly. If you are happy on the inside, then it surely will show on the outside. Not only with the way you dress, but your face, your smile, your tender look. Can a woman who puts on a grumpy face when her husband gets home be happy? Can a woman who goes out with a scowl and sloppily dressed be happy? How does a husband feel when he looks at his wife and sees a bitter, shabby woman? How must he feel? If you are feeling irritable because it's that time of the month, tell your husband. Make it very clear that the problem is hormonal (he will understand that he needs to be patient). Don't let him think he is the problem, or that you are unhappy with him. Appearance is not everything in my life, but if I love and value myself, why not take care of myself too? And I should do this even more now that I represent someone else.

When to use this tool: always. And find out what pleases your spouse regarding your appearance. Also communicate your preferences, but don't impose anything.

8. Never ridicule your partner

Don't do it privately or publicly. Being funny is not the same thing as making fun of someone. Beware of distasteful jokes. Don't expose your spouse's flaws and weaknesses to others. "Love *covers* all sins," says the wisdom of King Solomon.[20] Love hides the flaws of the other person. Even if your partner is wrong, show them your support rather than expose their mistakes. Teasing is disrespectful. Don't make comments that put down your spouse or reveal something that he has not yet made public. "Robert doesn't even know how to add. He only made it to the eighth grade." How do you think this will benefit your marriage? Sarcasm, irony, and disrespect are also fatal to any relationship. "You're going to write a to-do list? Since when are you any good with lists?" This attitude just shows that one spouse feels superior to other. Remember, love does not hurt.

When to use this tool: always. Be extra careful to implement this when the two of you are in the middle of a heated argument or among friends.

9. Drink some holy water

There's a story about a village where marital strife was rife. Tired of arguing with her husband, a wife went one day to seek advice from the village's wise man. "What must I do so my husband and I won't argue anymore?" she asked. The old man handed her a bottle of water and said, "This is holy water. Every time your husband starts an argument, drink some of this water—but keep it in your mouth for ten minutes before swallowing. And tell all your neighbors to do the same." Soon nobody argued in that village anymore! Opportunities to argue always come knocking at a couple's door. Remember, you don't have to open the door. If your spouse makes a comment that causes you to want to argue back, you can decide not to participate in this argument. You don't have to ignore the problem, but you can keep your cool, especially if you decide to control your tongue. Tempers will calm down,

---

[20] Proverbs 10:12.

and you will avoid an unnecessary argument, which would only push you both further apart. Isn't that better? Winning an argument is not as important as solving the problem. If you notice that your partner is getting aggravated, hold back and zip your lips. I'll never forget a couple from Singapore who attended our church meetings in London. On the day we offered a special prayer for their fiftieth wedding anniversary, we asked them what had been their secret to such a long-lasting life together. The husband replied: "When I get mad, she keeps quiet. When she gets mad, I keep quiet." This really does work.

When to use this tool: when you feel the urge to retaliate with harsh words.

10. Initiate conversation with a soft start-up

If you begin your conversation with a harsh tone, you will inevitably end up in an argument, even if there are many attempts to restore the peace afterward. Here are some classic examples: if the husband asks, "Do you need money?" (Good start) and the wife replies, "Just to pay the bills you didn't pay last week" (harsh response)—the daggers of accusation and sarcasm start to fly across the room. When the conversation starts well, chances are that it will finish well too. Choose your words carefully, do a mental test of what you are about to say, and then see if it sounds good. If you think that the other person may misinterpret you, choose other words to rephrase it. The conversation will have slowed down, and you will have had time to think and avoid stepping in a mess. If you notice that things have got out of line, take a deep breath, ask for forgiveness, and start again.

Cristiane:

One effective way is to tell your spouse how you feel about the problem, instead of treating him as if he is the problem. For example, if your husband is rude to you, it's not wise to call him rude, because you're starting off on an offensive note and attacking him, and he'll just react and only try to defend himself. But you can tell him how you feel when he speaks like that to you . . . "Honey, I feel bad when you answer me this way." See the difference? He isn't the one who makes you feel bad, it's the way he answers you. Focus on what you think and feel about the problem, instead of attacking the person involved in the problem.

When to use this tool: whenever you're dealing with a sensitive issue.

11. The filing cabinet of perpetual problems

I'm sorry to have to inform you, but there are certain flaws and things that irritate us about our partners that will never change. Perhaps he will always be messy. Maybe she'll always be a mama's girl. There are things in each of us that are part of our identity and will not change. Instead of getting frustrated and confronting the other person about it, take this problem and put it in the filing cabinet of perpetual problems—a little place in your brain that is reserved to remind you that it's useless to continue debating about this issue. The best thing for you to do is learn to deal with it. Put more laundry baskets in strategic places around the house. And even after you've done this, pick up the items that he still throws on the floor. Accept your wife's friendship with your mother-in-law—join them! If it's a tolerable problem that you are able to handle, then use this tool.

Stop trying to change the other person, because it won't happen. As we said in the beginning: you can only change yourself. Take the focus off your partner's flaws. Appreciate your spouse's qualities, and the contents in this filing cabinet will begin to have less and less importance in your relationship.

When to use this tool: when you identify a perpetual problem.

12. Delete the last ten seconds

From time to time we have to let some things go. One word that is said out of line, an unnecessary comment in a time of anger . . . Assess the situation and see if it's really worth getting into a heated argument about it. There will be times when your wife gets under your skin, and you'll want to explode, but remember: you don't *need to* explode. When you use a video camera and don't like what you just filmed, you go back and record new images to replace the old ones. In the same way, you can use this mental tool to "stop, rewind, and delete," by telling your spouse, "Okay, I'm going to pretend that I didn't see or hear what just happened. We started off on the wrong foot. Let's start over." This tool to erase the last ten seconds happens to be my own invention. I noticed that Cristiane sometimes acted on impulse or was driven by frustration, would say things she really didn't want to say, and would end up blurting out exactly how she was feeling. Instead of reacting angrily, I would—in a light-hearted manner—give her the signal that she was a little out of line. If she'd say something hurtful to me, I'd say, "Wait, let me rewind the tape right here. Okay, take 2. Action!" When she hears this, she understands that what she said was not appropriate and has a chance to rephrase it. Incidentally, if you failed to use the tool of "beginning with a soft start-up, you get another chance to use this tool and erase the last ten seconds. Use this tool light-heartedly and change the situation. Help the other person out, forgive, and give them another chance.

When to use this tool: when your partner steps out of line and you feel like strangling them with that line!

13. Don't let your body language cancel out your words

Communication experts say that over 90% of a conversation is nonverbal. Look at this number. More than 90%! Things like demeanor, tone of voice, eyes, facial expressions, and body language are responsible for almost all of what we convey. Our words carry less than 10% of our communication with another person. Saying, "Okay, I forgive you," while your face says (as you roll your eyes), "I'm only saying this because you asked, but I know you'll never change," does not make your forgiveness appear sincere. Besides facial and body language, something that speaks louder than your words is your recent behavior. If you say, "I'll change," yet have already promised it a hundred times and never did, your words will have no credibility for that person. So don't even think about complaining when your spouse doesn't believe you.

Pay attention to your nonverbal signals. It happens all the time in conversations. When a husband crosses his arms and says, "Okay, what do you want to say?" he's actually saying, "I'd rather be anywhere else than having this conversation. But don't you dare say that I didn't stop and listen." All this can be said without even saying a word. Body language and tone of voice that are more receptive are the secrets to good communication. Don't expect your conversation to turn out well when your demeanour is uptight and defensive, your tone is sarcastic, or you're sighing loudly. Always keep in mind that your partner is not an enemy, and your goal is to end the conversation well. Being open to dialogue is a prerequisite for this to happen. Try to communicate with your spouse in a loving, enjoyable, and nonthreatening manner. What both of you want is a healthy relationship, isn't it? You need to want it with all of your strength, and with all of your body—literally.

When to use this tool: in every conversation.

14. Rebuilding trust is a two-person job

If you've experienced unfaithfulness in your relationship, whether you're the culprit or the victim, you have to work hard and work together to rebuild trust. A common mistake is to blame only the one who was unfaithful: "It's all your fault. You're the one who gave me reason to be suspicious of you in the first place." We can easily believe that the offender is the only one who has to work to rebuild trust. But that is not the case. It takes both of you to make that happen.

This applies to any situation where trust has been broken. For example, a wife spends more than she should have, and now her husband no longer trusts her with money. In the case of unfaithfulness, the pain and suspicion will constantly haunt your thoughts, always asking, "Will it happen again?"

If you were unfaithful, you will have to do things differently to prove there has been a real change. Don't ask for an explanation as to why, just do it. It's the price of your unfaithfulness. Cut out the covert phone calls, stop deleting text or voice messages from your cell phone, allow your partner to have the passwords to your e-mail accounts, Facebook, and any other social sites. Some things have to stop being a part of your life, such as going out without saying where you're going or who you're with, keeping secrets, hiding information from your partner, or refusing to answer questions about your daily activities. This behavior will only continue to fuel distrust. For trust to be salvaged, the person who betrayed his or her partner needs to sear the word *transparency* into his or her mind. When you're transparent, you have nothing to hide, which eventually rebuilds your reputation as trustworthy. Be transparent in everything and don't complain about it. Don't come up with excuses such as, "What about my privacy?" or "I'm not doing it anymore, you have to trust me." You gave up your privacy on your wedding day. And if your spouse is giving you another chance and has forgiven you, it's transparency that will serve as a bridge to rebuild confidence, not your promises. It's like a citizen who commits a crime and is taken to court. A first-time offender may be eligible for probation. The judge will impose a few restrictions: stay within the county line, report to your probation officer on a weekly basis, etc.—but all is offered in exchange for not going to prison. The person who committed the crime and receives this kind of sentence is very relieved. He thinks, *I gotta toe the line now and report to my probation officer, but at least I'm not in jail!* He's grateful for the lucky break. It's the same thing for the person who betrays his or her spouse. They have to be thankful they're granted a second chance, and the only way to show it is to be transparent.

On the other hand, if you are the victim, stop reminding your partner of the past and refrain from constantly being suspicious. Don't assume things or jump to conclusions. Deal with the present facts. If your partner doesn't change, you may then have to tell him or her that there won't be a third chance. But don't keep dredging up the past. If he or she is committed to changing, don't play detective, investigating what doesn't need to be investigated, or implying that he or she is still cheating on you. It's extremely annoying and frustrating if we're trying hard to change, while others make it obvious that they don't believe that we've changed at all.

It is common for someone who's been cheated on to start seeing things that don't exist. It's merely fear taking control. Even so, be rational. Paranoia and suspicion won't help. Be smart, make plans, and be prepared for the possibility that the other person may not change—but leave plan B "in the drawer" and only take it out if necessary. This way you'll already know what to do if the worst were to happen.

Bury the past and drive a steamroller over it twenty times, so you won't even know where to find it. Don't turn back to grieve over it or to spit on its grave. Forget it. Help your partner in the process of rebuilding the relationship. It takes teamwork. Is it hard? Yes, nobody said it would be easy, but it's the only way for you to start rebuilding broken trust.

When to use this tool: in case of betrayal, lies, or any breach of trust in the relationship if you've decided to give yourselves a second chance.

15. Sleep on it

This is not a contradiction to tool number 1, where we advised you not to sleep on an unresolved problem, leaving it for the next day. That tool is to help you deal with problems that have *already occurred*. This one teaches you to deal with stress *before* the problem happens. Many problems in marriage arise from stressful situations in one or both partners. If you stay tuned to detect the problem BEFORE it happens, you can avoid it.

Watch your spouse's body language, tone of voice, and stress level. Give them enough space. People deal with stress differently. As a general rule, men need space and women need to talk. For sure, there are exceptions—there are women who also need silence and men who want to express their feelings. The important thing is to understand that if one is at a high level of irritability, it's useless trying to solve the problem right then and there.

This can also go along with the first rule: if the problem has already happened and you see that they are angry, it might be wiser to take a break to wait until he or she calms down. It's impossible to hold a conversation when people are acting on feelings and anger. This tool is similar to the "time-out" rule in basketball. When the team starts losing points, the coach requests a time-out, stops the game, and gathers the players to give them new instructions. It's an effective strategy to interrupt the momentum of the opponent.

Remember that there is an opponent to your marriage too. Don't leave an entryway for the devil. If you keep nit-picking at your spouse when he or she is angry, then you're doing your opponent a favor. Take a break. Agree to talk about it later on.

Though this tool is called "Sleep on it," it doesn't necessarily mean that you have to sleep—though a good night's sleep is a great way to restore mental and emotional health. It could just as well be a twenty-minute or one-hour break. The idea is to allow your partner to regain their strength and emotional balance.

When to use this tool: to detect signs of stress in your partner or yourself and take a break or do whatever helps calm you both down before problems arise.

16. Script and rehearse it for next time

In marriage we rarely have new problems. Disagreements about money matters or raising the children don't come around only once. It's normal for couples to deal with recurring problems from time to time, so what do you do when an old problem pops up again? First, resolve the conflict immediately, using the ten steps taught in chapter 6. Then ask yourself, "How can we prevent this from happening again?" or "What should we do if it does?" So as movie screenwriters plan what happens in the next scene, write your own "script" for the next time. What will you do when the same situation occurs? Decide what will happen, what each one's responsibilities will be, and make sure both of you agree on this. When a situation arises, both of you will know what to do, without losing your temper.

How does it work in practice? For example, a husband forgets his wedding anniversary. He's terrible with remembering dates, and his wife gets really irritated by it. And because he's forgetful, chances are that next year he'll forget it again. Some people are not really into remembering dates—it's a manufacturer's defect (as mentioned in tool 11). The couple must solve the problem of the wife's hurt feelings today, but they also must agree on how they'll handle this situation the next time.

The wife can write it down on her husband's calendar at the beginning of the year (simple, right?), remind him well in advance, post notes around the house . . . "But it's not the same! He needs to *want* to remember and surprise me!" she says. Understand one very important thing: our high expectations can lead us to want our partners to be just like us, and to place the same importance on the things that we do, but it doesn't always work that way. It's necessary to adjust our expectations to avoid recurring problems. There's a big gap between the real and ideal worlds. The wider the gap, the greater the frustration, and more problems happen. Forget about the ideal world and deal with your reality. Even if your reality is not satisfying, it's what you've got, and what you have to work with to achieve better results.

This tool applies to all situations. Many argue about how to raise the kids—one is strict while the other is more flexible. It doesn't take long for the kids to figure this out and start pitting one parent against the other to get their way. You both have to rehearse it for next time. Agree, for example, that the next time Dad says no, and the child runs to Mom in the hopes that she will override what Dad just said, Mom will instead stand by her husband's decision, even if she thinks that he was too harsh. You could discuss his judgment later when the kids aren't around to hear, but never let them see that you disagree with each other's decisions.

Another classic problem is money. You'd like your spouse to speak to you before spending so much money, but he or she doesn't. Now what? Some couples work it out and find common ground: "You can spend up to this amount, but anything above this, we need to talk over and decide together." This is how it's done. When a situation comes up, you already know how to deal with it, because you have a script.

Again, we go back to our business model. In business, you have to solve problems and prevent them from happening again, which is exactly what this tool is all about. In doing so, your problems will diminish considerably.

When to use this tool: when you see a problem rearing its head from the grave and you moan, "Here we go again . . ."

17. Protect your evenings

Breaking news! Evenings are a time to unwind. If you usually discuss problems and air grievances at this time, when your partner comes home from work, for example, you risk spoiling the mood for togeth-erness and intimacy—to put it bluntly, sex. One couple dealt with this by agreeing not to talk about problems after eight p.m. It worked for them, and you have to see what works for you. Just remember that if you're going to bed resenting each other or something that was said, you won't go to sleep as "one." This is the time of day to invest more in your relationship, as opposed to what many couples do who can't wait for their partners to get home to start complaining about the bills, or how the kids got into trouble with their teachers.

In The Love School "Lab" we had a couple with this problem. At dinnertime, she complained that he took too long to eat, but he asked her to give him some time because he wanted to relax and enjoy his meal. At one point, she said, "Why relax at dinnertime? There's so much to get done. I still need to clean up. Who has time to relax?" Because of the many things to be done at home, this couple's nights are often cha-otic. How could they invest in their intimacy if they can't relax during the only time of day they have together? Protecting your nights protects the hours leading up to intimacy. Many couples spend days, weeks, and even months without having sexual intercourse because they neglect their evenings. You're hoping to have a good night together, but because of one word out of place at dinnertime, your plans go down the drain. Don't forget that sex begins in the mind. When you're not careful with your behavior leading up to bedtime, you ruin the mood and blow your chances of a pleasant night between the sheets.

When to use this tool: every night and any other moment leading up to intimacy.

18. Rescue your partner

We can all feel overwhelmed at times. A wife may come home after a bad day at work and need to do a hundred household chores before she turns off the light to sleep. A caring husband will be sensitive to this and help ease the burden on her. He'll come to her rescue. "I'll take care of the groceries while you look at the kids' homework." "I'll fold the laundry and take the garbage out while you make dinner." Picking up after yourself also helps! In the same way, a wife should be a helper to her husband and make sure that she steps in when he's overwhelmed. Love means caring for the other person.

This goes right along with tool 17. If she comes home stressed out and just wants to unwind, her husband could be sensitive to her exhaustion and order a pizza so that she won't have to cook dinner. She feels valued and cared for. And if her husband is stressed out and she gives him some space to unwind, she is helping as well. If you notice that your spouse isn't feeling or doing what he or she normally would, just do it yourself. Don't make a mountain out of a molehill. Be there for them when they need it the most. This is a tool for emergencies. Help each other when one of you is taking on more than they can handle. Remember the question: *what does my spouse need from me right now?* Is it emotional support, medical care, guidance, practical help, or just keeping them company?

Cristiane:

I never liked demanding that Renato help me with the housework. I've always been the old-fashioned-housewife type, who doesn't want her husband to worry about anything. But one day, I couldn't take it anymore. I was overloaded with responsibilities at home and at work. We lived with two other couples, and when it was my turn to prepare lunch, I would cook for an army. Then I had to clean the kitchen and the rest of the house, besides preparing the afternoon snack and dinner . . . At the end of the day, I was beat! That was when I ended up in bed with a nasty bout of the flu.

I'll never forget what Renato did for me. He came to my rescue. He had always told me to hire someone to help with the housework twice a week, but because I didn't know anyone and was unsure if it would work out, I never tried. He called a cleaning service on his own and signed a two-week contract, organizing everything for me. I remember feeling so appreciated and valued by that simple gesture. He helped me when I needed it the most.

Housework is a subject that deserves special attention. Society has changed a lot, but the mentality of some people is still way behind. If you have constant arguments about the housework, make a list and agree on who is responsible for what. Who will take out the rubbish? Who will mow the lawn? Who will clean the bedroom? One of you? Both of you? The kids? Hire some help? In a company, everyone knows who does what, who makes the coffee, who cleans the conference room . . . Everything should be well defined. If everybody thinks that someone else will do it, then nobody does it. Set weekly, daily, and monthly tasks and decide who will do what. If you have kids, they can help too, and the family will be a team caring for their own home. Put the list up on the refrigerator so nobody will forget it. It's a practical way to solve these problems.

When to use this tool: whenever you notice that your spouse is overloaded or unable to do their normal duties.

19. Don't make personal attacks

"You're a liar," "You're rude," "You're stubborn." When you say things like that to your spouse, it's a sign that your relationship has descended to the lowest levels of disrespect—a trip it may not be able to come back from. Personal attacks mean that you've lost sight of who or what the real enemy is: the problem, rather than your partner. When you denigrate your spouse, you are cursing yourself, since it was you who chose to marry them!

Don't assume that your partner is lying. Two people can see the same scene and describe it in different ways. It doesn't mean that they are lying; they are just expressing their different points of view. Calling your spouse a liar for not agreeing with your version of the events can be a great injustice, so keep focused on the problem and don't attack their character. It's just not smart.

I cannot view Cristiane as the problem and attack her as if she were the problem herself. I need to learn to separate her from the problem. I hate the problem, but still love Cristiane. You need to remember that you're friends and are going to work together against the adversities that you are facing. You were both victims of a problem. You have now become its enemies, and both have the responsibility to figure out the solution, hand in hand.

When to use this tool: in any conversation, especially when your partner annoys you.

20. Do not project

If you've had a bad experience with your mother or father, or in a previous relationship, it's very easy to unfairly project your insecurities of the past onto your present partner. For example, a woman who was abused by her father can have unresolved resentments that cause her to overreact with all authority figures, even her husband. Or a man may have had a bad experience in his previous relationship and assumes that his present wife is going to be unfaithful just like his ex wife.

If I was cheated on in the past, and I project my traumatic experiences onto my wife, even the smallest thing that resembles the behavior of the other woman will cause me to attack her out of jealousy and feel suspicious, and my wife will never understand why. It's not her fault, but I'm already attacking her as if she had done the same thing. You project an image onto the other person as if he or she were at fault.

The example of a woman who was abused, and brings that trauma into her relationship, deserves a little more attention. She may be unable to have pleasure because of that abuse and feel disgusted with sexual intercourse. Her husband is not to blame, nor is the abused woman, but she is unable to deal with the situation. This problem has two sides: the projector and the screen that the image is being projected on to.

How can a traumatized person handle this situation? That's where the power of faith comes in. Psychologists and psychiatrists can certainly help, but human knowledge and medicine have their limits. However, faith in God has no limits and can heal the deepest wounds. God gives you the ability to forgive and even—literally—forget. He Himself uses that power for His own sake. It says in Isaiah 43:25, *"I, even I, am He who blots out your transgressions for My own sake; and I will not remember your sins."*

God, who has the ability to handle any situation, voluntarily decides not to remember our sins because He knows that it is no longer useful nor practical information. If a person repents and decides to change his life, He forgets about it and does not hold on to it. If you can't do it alone, seek help from God. It's also worth remembering that your spouse is not to blame for what happened to you in the past, so be fair. If you are dealing with someone who is going through this situation, be patient. Be aware of their emotional baggage and be considerate instead of reacting negatively. Use your head to help those who are still trapped by their emotions.

When to use this tool: as soon as you identify a traumatic event from the past as the root of a problem in your relationship.

21. Agree on how to raise the children

When there's no unified front on how to raise your children, you create a great deal of stress on your marriage, not to speak of confusing and frustrating your children. And never argue in front of the kids. If you disagree on something, discuss it in private. One of you can be very tough on the kids because of the way you were brought up, while the other may be more lenient, because of their past. Both methods may work, depending on the occasion, and you can make use of them both. Don't criticize your partner because they treat the children differently from you. Simply agree on how to do it in advance.

Children are children (and teenagers are basically overgrown children). They don't use their heads as much as their emotions because their minds are not yet fully developed. Unfortunately, your kids are not as emotionally mature as you'd like them to be. They'll get there, but until that happens, they need rules and discipline. They need boundaries, times to wake up, go to sleep, to sit at the table and eat with the family, to stick to their curfew (for teens), and to know when to speak and when to remain silent. Children will always try to push your buttons and test their boundaries. Of course, it's great to give them freedom to discover new things, but it's not healthy to let them do whatever they want. Parents are responsible for establishing rules through interacting and talking without aggression. Remember tool 16: script and rehearse it for next time. Children should not be given mixed messages.

If one of them starts to complain about either Mom or Dad, never criticize your spouse in front of your children. To prepare your children for the world, set boundaries and let them know about consequences and rewards. It's like driving a car. If you speed, you face the consequences of the law for your behavior: a hefty fine. If you have to pay a speeding ticket, you'll be more careful next time and drive under the limit. Many parents don't bother to tell their kids about the consequences for their behavior. I'm not talking about being too severe, but balanced—you don't want your children to be frightened. It's not about punishing them, but training them to help change their behavior. It can be done when they know the consequences for bad behavior and the rewards for good. So he got to school on time every day this week? Then he deserves to go to the movies over the weekend. That's life. If you do a great job, you expect your boss to recognize it, right? If this happens, you feel motivated to keep up the good work and do even better.

If your child is an adult and still lives with you, he can't be allowed to live in eternal teenager mode. He needs to contribute, help pay the bills, clean the house, and know the consequences for his choices. Unfortunately, many parents these days are raising bums because of the fear of being judged by a society that pits children against parents. They end up raising children who are totally unprepared for society. In the past, an eighteen-year-old guy was already a man, ready to take on his own responsibilities, and care for his own family. Today, the majority of eighteen-year-olds know nothing about life because their parents are letting society raise their children. You must establish a culture within your home—your own culture. Think about it, if there are rules even among gangsters (some of which are very strict), why can't you have rules too?

When to use this tool: daily, from the moment you decide to be parents, blending your parenting styles to arrive at an agreement on how to raise your children. Remember, preparing a human being for life is a big responsibility.

22. Remember that you're on the same team

What is more important, to be right or to be happy? For your marriage to do well or to prove yourself right? Individualistic people are terrible spouses. Couples have to learn to work as a team, because they are one. Sometimes you have to agree to disagree. A disagreement does not need to cause a fight. Stay united against the problems. Don't let them separate you. Never forget that the bottom line is that the whole team must win, and not just one of the players.

How does a team work? One of the fundamental skills in basketball is what is called "teamwork", when the players dribble and pass the ball up through the team until it reaches someone close enough to pop it into the basket. Note that the *personal* goal of each player is, of course, to score as many points as he can to become the team's leading scorer. And yet, he's ready to give up any personal goals for the success of the team. At that moment, it's not important which player individually scores the points, but their strategy is to get the best-positioned player to dunk that basket and boost their score. And if the last player to get the ball misses, the rest of the team doesn't tear him down, because they're all committed to the game and know that they need to keep working together.

Another aspect of a team is to recognize the strengths and weaknesses of each player. Each player plays in a position where he performs best, and they all complement one another. Cristiane is a better organizer and get-it-done person than I, and a great accountant too. She handles the finances. I'm a better strategist and planner; I am more into details. So we both combine our forces for the good of our marriage.

When to use this tool: from day one of your marriage, till death do you part. Especially when there is a disagreement, signs of selfishness, and problems that put up a wall between the two of you.

23. Money issues are really about trust issues

Prenuptial agreements, separate bank accounts, keeping income/expenditure information from your partner, among others, are signs that there are serious trust issues in your relationship. Find out why you can't trust your partner or why they can't trust you with money—and deal with that issue. Money-related issues have been cited as the number-one cause of divorce. Don't leave them unresolved. We're not talking here about a couple's financial problems, but the problems between you that are caused by money. A husband thinks his wife spends too much, or a wife complains that her husband can't save. You will argue until you're blue in the face if you don't deal with the root of the problem. How can I help my wife learn to spend more wisely? Taking the credit card away from her won't solve the problem. If I take away her credit card, she'll still have that problem plus one more: she'll feel hurt because of my attitude. I should ask myself, "What do I really want?" I don't want to take the card from her. I want her to help me trust her more. What are the options for dealing with the root of this problem? Will we have to sit down and do a household budget together? Will I have to give her an allowance so she can develop this skill? I, as head of the home, have to help her.

On the other hand, if you admit you can't control your spending, or have an addiction that wastes your money, and you don't know how to control it, accept help from your spouse for the sake of the team. By working together to solve this situation, you will find the best solution to budgeting and eliminate the source of stress in your relationship.

When to use this tool: if money issues have become a source of stress in your marriage, seek out the root of distrust

24. Don't interrupt your spouse

When you have a disagreement, let your spouse explain his or her point of view before you start talking. Resist the temptation to defend yourself or counterattack. This keeps the discussion on a rational level rather than on an emotional level. It is also important to focus on ONE POINT at a time. Do not finish talking about a subject until it has been resolved—only then move on to the next subject.

It's the problem of the two brains all over again. Men tend to do this naturally, talking out of that one particular box. Women already see all the connections to the problem. Soon, the argument has gone way off subject and has sunk to an irrational level. *What are we arguing about anyway?* Listen to your spouse first. Don't assume that you know what they're going to say before they've finished speaking. Don't think about your answer before you finish listening. It's not a competition. You don't have to defend yourself or win the debate. You must understand the problem rather than assume that you already do, and then talk. If you want to solve the problem, then let the other person speak.

Of course, this is not an excuse for those of you who can't stop talking and hog the conversation. I've seen plenty of couples where one is a born motor-mouth, and the other isn't. Arguments like these are annoying to watch when one dominates the conversation and the other can't even get a word in edgewise.

A good tip to avoid getting side-tracked is to write down the problems you want to solve. For example: *our house needs urgent repairs, and I've already told you about it several times.* Is that what you want to discuss? Then don't let the topic shift to your mother-in-law, the car, the dog, etc. Stay on that one subject only. Solve it, and then move on to the next.

When to use this tool: any time you feel like interrupting or taking over the conversation

25. Have a sense of humor

Encourage each other's sense of humor. Laugh as much as possible. If you don't make each other laugh regularly and often, consider the alternative! One of the things I know that keeps our marriage healthy is our sense of humor. It's a way to relieve the tension and make life fun. Marriage is a lifelong journey—make sure your journey is exciting, not boring.

Cristiane and I don't have a busy social life, but even so, it's never boring when we're together, precisely because both of us share this fun sense of humor. We joke with each other and make funny, light-hearted comments on things happening around us throughout the day. Some couples don't like to be together. The times they spend alone together are so boring that they end up getting tired and give up on each other. But for us, our daily interactions are so much fun that we can't stand being apart for too long.

We play pranks and have jokes that we'll never share with anyone else, and we know that nobody else could enjoy them because they're our own inside jokes. By the way, ladies, one more tip: men usually like to goof around and tell jokes. Some rarely talk about the same subjects their wives do. Men are generally much more serious. When they get together they don't talk about their hair or their clothes. Instead, they like to laugh. A husband can be extremely frustrated if he attempts to bring some fun into the relationship and his wife finds him silly and a nuisance (and even worse, when she tells him so). Then she complains that he watches too much television. What's fun about talking to someone who criticizes you for being at ease and who forces you to be uptight and serious all the time? Though you have different senses of humor, you must learn to appreciate the funny side of your husband. Being grumpy is not a sign of being responsible and mature. A recent survey by the accounting employment agency, Accountemps, which specializes in recruiting in the areas of finance and accounting, showed that 79% of CFOs believe that good humor is essential for employees to do well in their companies. If it were a sign of irresponsibility or flippancy, do you really think experienced executives would take it into consideration when hiring?

The benefits of a good sense of humor go far beyond the workplace and the health of your relationships. It is a known fact that an upbeat mood boosts the immune system, stimulates creativity, memory, and even helps reduce the sensation of pain, not to mention the increase in self-esteem! It's great when someone laughs with you. It creates bonds. Maybe your spouse would rather hang out with his friends because they laugh at his jokes! If you don't add anything to his or her times of fun, if you're a spoilsport and shrug off whatever your spouse or others have to say, why would anyone want to hang out with you?

When to use this tool: as long as you have breath in you. Just be careful not to offend your partner with a joke that he (she) does not appreciate or is said at inappropriate times.

26. Make sure you have his attention

This is a tool specifically for women. We mentioned earlier that due to the differences between men's and women's brains, women tend to multitask, while men tend to do one thing at a time. Women are able to do many things at the same time, but men do better focusing their attention on one thing at a time. So, women, when you want to say something very important to your husbands, make sure their eyes are on you and have disconnected from any other activity! But be careful. This often means that you will have to interrupt and take his focus off what he is doing to focus on you. Choose the right time, speak gently— and still be prepared that you might have to remind your "clueless guy" again later about what you talked about, if it's really that important.

When to use this tool: whenever you need your other brain to register something important.

27. Keep romance alive

Marriage is not based on emotion. Instead, it's hard work and perseverance, but a little romance goes a long way. It's important for both partners in a marriage to constantly do special things for each other.

If we're not careful, our job, the kids, and other responsibilities and pressures will take up all our time. Make sure you have "just us" time. Taking work home on a regular basis, spending hours in front of the TV, allowing the kids to take all your time and attention are examples of behaviors that cause couples to grow apart. You need your "just us" time—make sure you plan for it.

Hollywood wants us to believe that romance has to be complicated, elaborate, and expensive, but it doesn't. Romance can be defined as "doing something out of the ordinary that shows your love for the other person." It doesn't have to be a big thing. Most of the time romance has to do with the small things. Men, you may not consider yourself to be romantic, but it's not that hard. Just be spontaneous. You don't have to spend a lot of money to be romantic. Here are some ideas: call your wife in the middle of the day and ask her how she is. Leave a note or a card like the ones you used to write when you were dating (you can put it under her pillow or by her toothbrush, or tuck it into her suitcase when she's traveling). Giving flowers nowadays can seem cheap and doesn't always work. Too many guys pick up a cheap bunch of carnations at the supermarket on the way home and think they're winning major points, but their wives see the lame attempt as just that—lame! If you get her flowers, find the ones you know she loves, ones with a special meaning to her. You can also turn off the phones, make popcorn, and rent a movie that she likes to watch while snuggling on the couch (no falling asleep during the movie. That definitely is not romantic). Finally, be creative. Do something different, but simple, that shows you think of your spouse, even in the most mundane moments. Your homework is to do something romantic for your partner this weekend. Let's get going!

When to use this tool: at least once or twice a month, and whenever the routine of married life turns boring. This is a maintenance tool. Surprise your spouse.

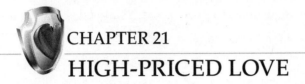

CHAPTER 21

HIGH-PRICED LOVE

A couple's fiftieh anniversary was approaching, and they decided to celebrate. When asked about their secret to long-term harmony, the husband replied:

"You know the heel on a loaf of bread? Well, that's my favorite part, but every morning for fifty years I've given her the heel."

When his wife was asked the same question, she said:

"You know the heel on a loaf of bread? Well, I hate the heel! But for fifty years I've eaten the heel without complaining . . ."

This small example reveals a big secret of what should be the foundation of every marriage. In one word: sacrifice. For fifty years he gave up what he liked out of love for her, and she gave up what she liked for him. Think of the foundation of a house or building. It keeps that structure standing. The same goes for sacrifice in marriage. When people look at a couple from the outside, what they don't see is that their happiness is a direct result of the sacrifices they make for each other.

NINETEEN YEARS IN A COMA

Ever since hearing about this couple, I've not been able to forget their example. For me, it's one of the best examples of what love truly is: sacrificial love. Jan Grzebski was a Polish railroad worker. In 1988 he suffered a blow to the head while trying to connect two railroad cars together and fell into a coma. Doctors gave up on him, especially after discovering he had a brain tomur. Their opinion was that he would never recover or even survive much longer. Gertruda Grzebska, Jan's wife, ignored those words of defeat and decided to take him home and care for him on her own.

Still in a coma, Jan could not speak, walk, communicate, or interact in any way. The relationship they had enjoyed was now over. The strong husband who had always been at her side was now a baby, totally dependent on her as his caregiver. She finished raising their children on her own, while struggling to keep her husband alive. He could only do the most basic activities, such as breathing, swallowing, and opening and closing his eyes. And yet she would get extremely angry whenever anyone suggested euthanasia (arguing that it would "end that suffering") because she believed the right thing was to give him a chance to recover. Every day Gertruda spoke to her husband as though he could hear her and kept turning him so he didn't develop bedsores—common in bedridden patients, which can lead to deadly infections. The children grew up, got married, and gave them grandchildren. Gertruda took her husband to all major family get-togethers as if he were able to participate.

Tireless Gertruda received her reward in 2007. After nineteen years in a coma, Jan finally awakened at the age of sixty-five. Doctors credited his recovery to his wife, who chose the hardest path. Jan had an even stronger connection with her now because he remembered that she was at his side when he most needed her. She did what was right and best for him, giving up her own life to take care of her husband, without demanding anything in return. She believed even when doctors didn't. She waited, persisted . . . and was rewarded.

During the coma, Gertruda described her husband as "a living corpse," yet she still remained by his side. There were no emotions in what she did or romance. It was pure sacrifice, true love—but can you think of anything more romantic? No love story is more beautiful than those that involve sacrificial love. Gertruda received a well-deserved medal of honor from the president of Poland for her dedication and sacrifice, reinforcing how rare it is to find this kind of love nowadays.

Looking at the harsh reality that Gertruda endured for nineteen years, the inevitable questions are: what would you have done in her place? What kinds of problems have you had to face in your marriage? Will you give up on your spouse?

Only sacrificial love overcomes all things. It's a high-priced, genuine love.

Beware of cheap imitations.

LOSE TO WIN

Sacrifice is the way to put everything we've taught you throughout this book into practice. In fact, every successful person is familiar with the concept of sacrifice. In any area of life, when a person conquers something of great value, performs great deeds, or obtains victories, they will have had to cross the bridge of sacrifice. This is the shortest path to success. But, of course, it is not the easiest.

What is sacrifice? Picture it being extremely cold, and I have two coats, and the person next to me is shivering. I give him one coat and keep the other one. This would not be a sacrifice; it would simply be giving. But if I only have one coat and give that coat to that other person, now I'm sacrificing. Sacrifice is giving up something now because you are certain that you will gain something of much greater value in the future. At times, this thing of greater value is your clear conscience, knowing that you did the right thing, not what you felt like doing. This is what Gertruda did.

True love is marked by sacrifice. It's expensive. As we've already mentioned, love is not an emotion. It includes feelings, but it is not defined by them. The world mixes love with emotions in a recipe that's pretty indigestible: measure out the word "love," the desire to be together, jealousy, greed, sexual desire . . . stir them all together, then heat it up with music, movies, and art, and then sell it to people as "love." But that's not love. It's counterfeit. The combination of two things is what defines love:

Doing what is right for the other person. I have to be fair to the person I love. I have to do right by her, no matter what I do or do not feel, think or do not think, or how much it's going to cost.

Sacrifice. If your love is simply a good feeling, it will not survive the storms. The only love that outlasts any problem is a love that's not based on feelings, but on sacrifice. Those who say "our love ran out" do not know what love is. True love never ends.

The selfishness of present-day couples blocks them from putting this concept into practice, telling them that they'll get hurt when they sacrifice. But those who've chosen to walk the path of true love have no regrets.

I don't want you to equate marriage with suffering or carrying a heavy cross for all eternity. Sacrifice is not an end in itself. It's simply a means of achieving something greater. It is like a person who applies for a challenging new job that pays three times his current salary. If he doesn't sacrifice his free time to study, take a course or brush up on his skills, he can't expect to get that job. Start sacrificing for your marriage, and you'll have a wonderful relationship of peace, understanding, companionship, and loyalty . . . one that more than makes up for all the suffering you had to go through in the beginning. Without a doubt you'd do it all over again after seeing the results. Try it.

You may ask, "But aren't there limits? What if my spouse never gives back. Am I stuck with him for the rest of my life?"

Obviously some people don't want another person's love. Some even reject God's love. So, having a relationship with these people is impossible. Not even God forces people to love or follow Him. He sacrificed for everyone, but not everyone accepts His sacrifice or the conditions they need to meet to have a relationship with Him.

Love should be unconditional when it comes to understanding your partner's weaknesses. But when it comes to a relationship or marriage, it should never be unconditional. For two people to live together, certain prerequisites must be met. I love my wife, but if she cheats on me, I don't see how I could possibly continue a relationship with her. I know she feels the same way about me. Faithfulness is a prerequisite for our marriage to work. Would I give her another chance if there were sincere repentance? Maybe. Every case is different, and everyone has his own faith and limitations. But one thing is certain: a good relationship requires involvement from both parties. If the other person doesn't want you, then your sacrifice may be better spent on someone else.

HOW DO WE APPLY THIS TO MARRIAGE?

I am going to list some examples (there are many more) of sacrifice in marriage so you can better understand when and how this applies:

The sacrifice of communication: I had to learn to communicate more with Cristiane. Going to her to start a conversation wasn't something I normally did. I was frequently tired and enjoyed being quiet. I would communicate in one-word sentences. Out of love, I sacrificed this behavior and began to answer her questions. Even now when she asks me questions, I find that I have to force myself to answer her because I don't always feel like talking. I see no sense in talking about certain things, but I think to myself: *What I feel doesn't matter. I'm going to do what's important to her.* When a husband is the quiet-type and his wife is very talkative, it's a sacrifice for him to be talkative with his wife. On the other hand, nobody can stand a wife who talks too much, is demanding, imposing, and pushy. Her husband will find her to be a much nicer person if she makes the sacrifice to slow down and be less demanding.

If both do this, they'll create a healthy balance. If only one does it, only half of the problem will be solved . . . but the other half will be positively affected, and the other half of the problem will also be solved sooner or later.

The sacrifice of humility: This happens when you swallow your pride, give in, and admit that your partner is right. This is a sacrifice because it hurts, and since you do not want to feed your hard heart, you sacrifice your pride and admit your mistakes.

Sacrificing your free time: It's a sacrifice when your wife likes to go out and you take her out simply to please her, or when your husband doesn't like to go out and you stay home with him and resist complaining about it. Your husband loves football, but you can't understand what is so interesting about a bunch of men chasing a ball. And yet you sit next to him and try to learn how to enjoy it, seeing it through his eyes because it's important to him. Just seeing your spouse happy will make it fun for you.

The sacrifice of sex: When you look at sex in a selfish way and refuse to sacrifice during it, your goal is simply your own pleasure, nothing more. When you learn how to sacrifice, you'll be able to put your partner's pleasure above yours. Then neither of you will ever feel ignored because your goal is to please the other person, and you'll not be satisfied until he or she is. Mutual pleasure can only be found through sacrifice.

The sacrifice of irritability: There are times when we need to simply ignore annoying habits. Think about it: compared to all the other positive aspects of the relationship, that habit is totally insignificant. You won't make a big deal out of a small thing.

The sacrifice of emotions: This might be one of the greatest sacrifices because it has to do with the heart. Knee-jerk reactions and emotion cause couples to explode and hurt each other, which feeds each other's anger, and then they end up sleeping in separate rooms. We have to sacrifice our emotional instincts that lead us to act before we think. I will not allow my emotions to persuade me to insult my wife. I have to respect her. Neither will I annoy her with endless complaints, which lead to pointless and unnecessary arguments. Cristiane stopped complaining to me and began complaining to God, asking Him to change my behavior. She sacrificed her emotions and relied on God.

The sacrifice of goals: When your personal goals exclude your marriage, it is often necessary to sacrifice them. Whenever we place our personal goals above our relationship, it damages it. This is why many celebrity marriages end in divorce. If your career is more of a priority than your marriage, your partner will feel that he or she is simply an add-on to your life. It's hard to put up with a situation like this for very long. Both of you should sacrifice your personal goals and find common ones.

The sacrifice of friendships: If a friend has a negative influence on your marriage, or makes your spouse feel uncomfortable or suspicious, you should sacrifice that friend for your marriage. Friends of the opposite sex or relatives who cause jealousy should be kept at a distance.

FORGIVENESS: THE GREATEST OF ALL SACRIFICES

If your spouse has caused you a lot of pain and disappointment, and you want to move forward in the relationship, you need to press the "reset" button. When your computer crashes, restarting it will frequently take care of the problem, right? Likewise, for your marriage to work you have to press the reset button by forgiving.

Forgiving may be something we do not *feel* like doing. What we feel like doing is punishing the other person. We're tempted to think that forgiveness means that the other person will never suffer the consequences of their actions. And so we hold a grudge as a way of exacting revenge. There is a saying: refusing to forgive is like drinking rat poison and waiting for the rat to die. Think about it. The rat's not going to die! You drank the poison; you're going to die. The rat's going to be free, running back and forth, up to no good and gnawing at everything he comes across. Who loses in this scenario?

Bitterness enslaves. It's a burden that is not consistent with intelligence. Why lug around an unnecessary burden? The other person has already gotten over the past and is looking ahead, but you're at a standstill obsessing over the past. Forgive, not because the other person deserves it, but because you don't want to be burdened with it. Bitterness is emotional garbage. When you feed bitterness, you're eating garbage. It's as if you're eating rotten food, walking around with a backpack of rancid food that you plan to eat for dinner, and whenever anyone tells you to get rid of it, you tighten your grip.

I know exactly what this feels like. I was bitter toward a person in my family who was partially responsible for my parents' separation. As a teen I made a promise to myself to pay this person back for what she had done. When I began attending church and heard the pastor say that we had to forgive our enemies, my first thought was: *You don't know the person who destroyed my family. It's easy for you to say because you don't know what I went through.* Maybe this is what's going through your mind as you read about forgiveness. I didn't understand it at first, but over time I realized that she was not being hurt by my bitterness. I was being hurt. When I understood that I needed to forgive for my own good, I got interested in finding out how this could be done, since I really didn't feel like doing it.

SO . . . HOW DOES A PERSON FORGIVE?

The first thing to know about forgiveness is that it's not a feeling; it's a decision. Deciding to forgive was not difficult, since I understood it was the right thing to do. I just needed the ability to move on. The second step was to start praying for her. Many who continue to carry emotional garbage around claim that they pray for their enemies, yet what they say in their prayers doesn't help. You can't expect to get rid of bitterness when you pray: *Lord, make John pay for what he did*. That's not praying for your enemies! That prayer is anger that God will not listen to. The Bible tells us to bless those who persecute us[21]. . . . *Bless and do not curse*. That's how we should pray.

At first my prayers were insincere. I would start off praying for her, asking God to bless her, but what I really wanted Him to do was strike her in the head with a lightning bolt. Ignoring my desire to see her torn into a million pieces, I continued to pray. Over time, the stone that had been my heart shattered, and I started seeing her in a different light. Prayer helped me change the way I looked at her. That's when I took the third step: I began to look forward. I realized that I had to be practical. Looking back was not smart. What was done was done. If she needed to pay for what she had done, that would be God's problem; I had nothing to do with it. I also realized that I had many flaws and had no right to demand perfection from her, because I wasn't perfect either. If God, who is perfect, looked at me with the same severity that I looked at her, I would be completely lost! But if I welcomed His forgiveness, how could I not forgive as well? *And forgive us our debts as we forgive our debtors*.[22]

---

[21] Romans 12:14
[22] Matthew 6:12.

When you do not forgive, you can't even pray The Lord's Prayer. Have you thought about it that way? It's unfair for me to want something that I'm not willing to give.

This is the difference between genuine and emotional love. Our hearts are the center of our emotions and will always insist on doing what they feel like doing rather than what needs to be done. You may know that the right thing to do is talk to your spouse, but you may not feel like doing it. Your heart will quickly come up with an excuse: *Why do I have to talk to him? He's the one who was wrong!* But when we use our heads, take charge of our hearts, and refuse to live by emotions, we'll do the right thing even when it's not what we want to do.

It's a constant war. I can't predict what I'm about to feel. No one has control over that. Emotions come like waves. But I can control my head; I can determine what I think and how I react to that feeling. Whenever my heart is using my own emotions against me, I have to use my intelligence.

Does this sound impossible? You do this every morning, especially Monday mornings. You don't feel like getting out of bed. You want more sleep. You press the snooze button and are rewarded with an extra five minutes of dreamland. But when the alarm goes off again, your head says: *You can't miss work. You can't be late again. Get up and go to work.* So you get up and drag yourself to the bathroom against your own will. If needed, you even jump into the shower before the water's heated up just to show your heart who's the boss. Resigned to your resolve, your heart gives up insisting, and you're able to eat breakfast and go to work. If you didn't do this, you wouldn't have a job, right? This is how to win the battles in your marriage. Yes, it's a sacrifice, but it's absolutely doable. Everything that's really nice is expensive.

TASK:

What sacrifices do you need to start making, or continue making, for your relationship?

 /BulletproofMarriage

On our Facebook page
fb.com/BulletproofMarriage
post: *I don't want cheap love, and so I've decided to sacrifice.*
#Bulletproofmarriage

 @BulletproofMate

Tweet: *I don't want cheap love, and so I've decided to sacrifice.*
#BulletproofMarriage
@BulletproofMate

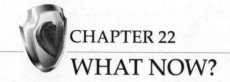

CHAPTER 22
WHAT NOW?

We truly hope that you've woken up to the fact that marriage in the twenty-first century is not what it used to be. We're living in a new world, surrounded by a culture of apathy, and a new set of threats that did not exist only a number of years ago. For those who still want to get married and stay married, bulletproofing your relationship is no longer a luxury, it's a necessity.

What we've done up to this point in this book is exactly the opposite of what the world is doing. While the world talks about being liberal, progressive, modern, and sleeping around—we've gone right back to the beginning of all things, to the Garden of Eden, and traced the footsteps of men and women right up to the present time. We've discovered what's the essence of marriage, what works, that love is marked by what we do, not by how we feel, what are the particular curses affecting men and women, how they affect their relationship, and how to effectively deal with them. We also learned about the fundamental differences between the sexes and their inherent conflicts. We learned to identify the root of a problem and solve it by using reason instead of emotion. We spoke about dozens of practical tools that can be applied to your marriage on a daily basis, in order to solve and prevent problems.

You learned a little about Cristiane and me, and we hope that our struggles and experiences have in some way helped you to better understand your own marriage. We tried to give you a realistic idea of what marriage is, revealing its difficulties but also its joys and beauty. A happy marriage takes work, yes—but the payoff is worth all the effort! We want to raise the flag of true love, challenge the myths and misinformation that plague today's relationships, and show that you can be married and very happy. We honestly believe that only happily married couples experience complete happiness. This is why we were created. It is possible. Do not let anyone tell you otherwise.

Cristiane and I do not consider ourselves "lucky." Our happy marriage is the result of our decisions, which often went against our feelings, and the practice of spiritual intelligence, which is obedience to the advice of God. If we had not done this, and continued doing what we had done in the beginning, we would just be another statistic. Anyone—including you—who puts this advice into practice, can have a happy marriage. This should not be taken lightly. We are here because we've lived out our faith. Intelligence refuses to believe that a successful love life is possible without the True Love—God. Everything you want to accomplish in life, not only in your marriage, is possible through faith in Him—even the answers you have not found in this book. And so, in response to the question "What now?" we would advise:

Seek a close relationship with the God of the Bible through the Lord Jesus. He doesn't want you to become religious, but rather to develop a relationship with Him.

Plus, we are absolutely certain that the principles and practical lessons you learned in this book work. They are not always easy to put into practice, but they work. Difficult is not the same as impossible, and just because there may be a delay in seeing results, that does not mean they won't come. Be patient and persistent. Don't expect a complete change within a matter of days, and don't demand that of your partner. Start with a first step and continue working at it.

We think you should focus on some key points: one, two, or three main points that touched you the most, and that you know require urgent attention. Work on these points until they become a part of your life. Then go back to the other chapters and work on other areas. It's like changing your eating habits. You may want to lose weight, but you know that you can't drastically cut down your calories and starve because that won't work. But if you change your diet gradually and exercise more often, the result will come naturally and it'll be permanent. Stay focused on change and continuous effort, and you'll reach your goal. Do not give up. As the saying goes, a thousand-mile journey begins with a single step. The results will come with practice.

Cristiane and I want to be a positive influence in your life and would like to suggest some steps that can bring results for your relationship and help others. Here they are:

Review the sections of this book that caught your attention, or those that you feel you need to understand more thoroughly. You'll be surprised by how much this will help you to absorb and retain the most important points. It will help you remember what you learned and how to act in the future.

If you did not complete all of the tasks, there's still time. Go back and work on them. Do not underestimate the power of implementing them. Whether you feel like it or not, do it!

Keep in touch with us through our websites and blogs. We would love to receive your feedback and continue to help you. Leave a comment, watch our videos, tell us your experiences. This is also how you can stay informed of what we're up to, our calendar of events around the world:

- Blogs: renatocardoso.com and cristianecardoso.com
  Facebook: fb.com/BulletproofMarriage
- Twitter: @BulletproofMate; Renato @brcardoso; Cristiane
  @criscardoso
  E-mail: book@bulletproofmarriage.org

Do something nice for someone else by giving him or her a copy of this book. If someone you know is about to get married and needs to learn to do things the right way, get them a copy. If you know someone who's married and needs to bulletproof their relationship, give them this book as a present. They will thank you and will most probably never forget you.

We suggest that you keep your copy of this book and read it again in six months. Change takes time and requires persistence. So, go to your calendar now and make this note six months from today:"Reread *Bulletproof Marriage* book."Those who do this will see much greater results.

Happy bulletproof marriage!

Renato & Cristiane Cardoso

ACKNOWLEDGMENTS

Above all, to the inventor of marriage—God. And for those who may not understand: the fact of creating man and woman, so different from each other, and making them live together might seem like a bad joke. But He always knows what He's doing. We thank Him for gifting to us our spouse's life in union. Renato would not be Renato without Cristiane, and in like manner, Cristiane would not be Cristiane without Renato. It's hard to explain.

To the problems we have had to go through during our marriage. They have been hard, but they have also been our greatest teachers.

To Bishop Macedo and to Mrs. Ester, perhaps the most solid and happy couple that we have met who have influenced us the most. Thank you for your insights, many of which are woven throughout this book.

To David and Evelyn Higginbotham, who have helped us develop this work in Texas, always with excellent insight.

To Ágatha Cristiana and Raquel Parras, who have researched, edited, read, and reread this book more times than a person should have.

And to all of our team and students from Bulletproof Marriage and from *The Love School*. Your contribution to this book has been enormous. Rejoice with us!

Renato and Chritiane Cardoso

BIBLIOGRAPHY

Introduction

"Marriage and Divorce Statistics." *epp.eurostat.ec.europa.eu. Eurostat European Commission,* 8 January 2013. Web. 12 August 2013. http://goo.gl/6ElGsG. "Most Babies Born out of Marriage by 2016, Trend Suggests." *bbc.co.uk.* BBC, 11 July 2013. Web. 12 August 2013. http://goo.gl/u88WTF.

Chapter 1

Leff, Alex. "'Til 2013 Do Us Part? Mexico Mulls 2-year Marriage." Reuters. N.p., 29 September. 2011. Web. 12 August. 2013. http://reut.rs/1ctnzda.

DeParle, Jason, and Sabrina Tavernise. "For Women Under 30, Most Births Occur Outside Marriage." Nytimes. com. *The New York Times,* 17 February 2012. Web. 12 August 2013. http://goo.gl/20i3q.

Wiley-Blackwell. "Do children need both a mother and a father?" *ScienceDaily.* 28 January 2010. Web. 12 August 2013. http://goo.gl/ZPeYp.

Paul, Pamela. "Are Fathers Necessary?" *The Atlantic.* Atlantic Media, 8 June 2010. Web. 12 August 2013. http://goo.gl/frSb4w.

Stevens, John. "The Facebook Divorces: Social Network Site Is Cited in 'a THIRD of Splits'" *Mail Online.* Associated Newspapers Ltd, 30 December 2011. Web. 12 August 2013. http://goo.gl/D8VZC.

Gardner, David. "The Marriage Killer: One in Five American Divorces Now Involve Facebook." *Mail Online.* Associated Newspapers Ltd, 2 December. 2010. Web. 12 August 2013. http://goo.gl/qOUF2.

"Internet Pornography Statistics" – TopTenReviews. TechMedia Network, n.d. Web. 12 August. 2013. http://goo.gl/sVnAk.

"Statistics on Pornography, Sexual Addiction and Online Perpetrators." And Their Effects on Children, Pastors and Churches. TechMission, n.d. Web. 12 August 2013. http://goo.gl/GUqHql.

"ChristiaNet Poll Finds That Evangelicals Are Addicted to Porn." Marketwire. N.p., 7 August 2006. Web. 12 August. 2013. http://goo.gl/OKfAYB.

"Wounded Clergy: Ministers Are Not Immune to Compulsive Sexual Behavior!" Hopeandfreedom.com. Hope & Freedom Counseling Services, n.d. Web. 12 August 2013. http://goo.gl/5FuKoQ.

Sampaio, Rafael, and Luisa Ferreira. "Women are the majority in universities around the world" R7.com. Record TV Network, 26 November 2010. Web. 12 August 2013. http://goo.gl/FDvS8b.

Cardoso, Rodrigo, and Carina Rabelo. "Women Are Cheating More." ISTOÉ - Independente. Terra.com, n.d. Web. 12 August. 2013. http://goo.gl/2xMtTl.

"Pornography Statistics." *Familysafemedia.com*. Family Safe Media, n.d. Web. 12 August 2013. http://goo.gl/n0i7o8.

Chapter 2

Covey, Stephen. "Part 1." *The 7 Habits of Highly Effective People*. London: Simon & Schuster, 1999.

Chapter 4

Fahmy, Miral. "In Love? It's Not Enough to Keep a Marriage, Study Finds." Reuters.com. Ed. Nick Macfie. Reuters, 14 July 2009. Web. 12 August 2013. http://goo.gl/hk2x1Z.

The Barna Group. "New Marriage and Divorce Statistics Released." *Barna.org*. The Barna Group, 31 March 2008. Web. 12 August 2013. http://goo.gl/nxv3Ca.

Chapter 6

"5 Whys." *Wikipedia.org*. Ed. Wikipedia. Wikipedia, n.d. Web. 12 August 2013. http://goo.gl/SPT3vd.

Chapter 7

Seckel, Al, and John Edwards. "Franklin's Unholy Lightning Rod." *Evolvefish.com*. Evolvefish, n.d. Web. 12 August 2013. http://goo.gl/yh8Svq.

Chapter 8

"Soulmate." *Wikipedia.org*. Wikipedia, n.d. Web. 12 August 2013. http://goo.gl/QerMuB.

Chapter 15

Gray, John, Dr. "The Male vs. the Female Brain." *Thirdage.com*. Thirdage, 27 April 2007. Web. 12 August 2013. http://goo.gl/Z4c02ZBrainfacts.org. Brain Facts—A Public Information Initiative of The Kavli Foundation, the Gatsby Charitable Foundation, and the Society for Neuroscience, n.d. Web. 12 August. 2013. http://goo.gl/TlwajV

Brizendine, Louann. *The Female Brain*. New York: Morgan Road, 2006.Gungor, Mark. *Laugh Your Way to a Better Marriage: Unlocking the Secrets to Life, Love, and Marriage*. New York: Atria, 2008.

Chapter 16

hooks, bell. *Feminist Theory*. Cambridge, MA: South End, 2000. 26.Brasil.gov.br. "1977 Divorce Law." *Brasil. gov.br*. Jornal Do Brasil, n.d. Web. 12 August 2013. http://goo.gl/OONnRD (Divorce & Feminism).

Chapter 17

Merriam-Webster Online Dictionary. "Husband." *Merriam-webster.com*. Merriam-Webster Online, n.d. Web. 12 August 2013. http://goo.gl/2UGfzn.

Chapter 20

"Avoid Divorce with 5:1 Ratio." *Marriagegems.com*. Marriage Gems, 25 July 2011. Web. 12 August 2013. http://goo.gl/tmaANL.

"Accountemps Survey: Executives Say Humor Is Key Part of Cultural Fit." *Accountemps.com*. Accountemps, 31 January 2012. Web. 12 August. 2013. http://goo.gl/gAnqTR.